FREEMASONRY
& FRATERNAL SOCIETIES

FREEMASONRY
& FRATERNAL SOCIETIES

DAVID HARRISON and FRED LOMAX

Lewis Masonic

This impression 2015

ISBN 978 0 85318 496 6

Published by Lewis Masonic

an imprint of Ian Allan Publishing Ltd, Addlestone, Surrey, KT15 2SF

Printed in Wales

Visit the Lewis Masonic website at www.lewismasonic.co.uk

CONTENTS

List of Tables

List of Illustrations

Acknowledgements

The authors would like to thank a host of people for assisting with the researching and writing of this book. First and foremost, we would like to thank our families for all their support, and the publisher for offering us the opportunity to write the work, with a special mention to Martin Faulks and Philippa Faulks. Many thanks are also due to various leading members of the fraternal societies for the valuable information they have supplied: Paul Eyres, Provincial Corresponding Secretary, South Yorkshire and North Derbyshire, Independent Order of Oddfellows; Andy Baker, Grand Tyler 2005, RAOB, GLE; Roger M.L. Williams of Moose International British Headquarters; James Jack, Secretary of Adelphi Bluebell Lodge No. 4 of the Free Gardeners; Kai Hughes for his information on the AOD, and many more that gave their time in answering questions and supplying us with information. All photographs are by Fred Lomax unless otherwise stated.

ABBREVIATIONS USED IN THIS BOOK	
AOD	Ancient Order of Druids
AOF	Ancient Order of Foresters
BPOE	Benevolent and Protective Order of the Elks
IOF	Independent Order of Foresters
IOGT	Independent Order of Good Templars
IOR	Independent Order of Rechabites
LOOM	Loyal Order of the Moose
OTO	Ordo Templi Orientis
RAOB	Royal Antediluvian Order of Buffaloes
RIBA	Royal Institute of British Architects
UGLE	United Grand Lodge of England

FOREWORD

The idea for this book came about back in 2012 when David and I were looking through material in the possession of the Wigan & District Association for Masonic Research, of which I am the Secretary, for his book *The Liverpool Masonic Rebellion and the Wigan Grand Lodge*. I happened to mention that I had written a paper on other fraternal societies and how similar they were to Freemasonry. The paper was to be included in my book *Fred's Five Minute Talks*: although many of those societies had passed into the annals of history some had survived, and we felt that their stories would make interesting reading not just for Freemasons but for members of other societies as well.

Fred Lomax, Past Provincial Junior Grand Warden for both West Lancashire & East Lancashire Provinces, and Provincial Grand Orator for East Lancashire.

This book aims to be not just a quick guide to other Orders, fraternal societies and clubs but also an examination of the similarities between them and Freemasonry. Many of the Orders discussed here were clearly modelled on Freemasonry, and these similarities can be seen in the many photos displayed throughout the book, both in the aprons, sashes and jewels and in the rituals and ceremonies that have been meticulously copied and presented here from original sources.

Research for the book also led to a comparison between the working-class societies and the gentlemen's clubs of the period, many of which also had members who were Freemasons. Indeed, my first experience of Freemasonry was when I worked at a financial organisation called United Friendly Insurance in the late 1980s, when the branch manager began a conversation about it. United Friendly had begun its life as a mutual benefit society, and had bought out a number of smaller benefit clubs throughout its history. The same discussion with the manager also gave me an introduction to and inspired an interest in friendly societies, and how their history was somewhat entwined with that of Freemasonry. Another job followed at Liverpool Victoria Insurance, a friendly society that had begun in the early Victorian era, which sparked my interest further.

When I finally became a Freemason in 1998 another memorable conversation I had with a senior member of the lodge introduced me to the Foresters: we were talking about initiations and he mentioned that his father had been a member of the Foresters in Leigh, an industrial town in the north-west of England. On his initiation he had entered a room 'above a pub' and, as he walked through the door, a man with a drawn bow and arrow stood at the other end aiming directly at him. It was a vivid mental image that came back to me when I was co-writing this book with Fred Lomax.

These two conversations – one about the financial aspect of friendly societies, and the other about the more ritualistic elements – enabled me to realise what these societies were all about during a time of rapid change and intense industrialisation: the financial part offered protection and cover in times of hardship and sickness, while the ritual part offered a sense of bonding and shared experience. Both were essential to some men as they strove to survive in an ever-developing community with little or no assistance from either the state or their place of employment.

Dr David Harrison, history lecturer and Master Mason.

INTRODUCTION

'Box Clubs' had been appearing in the UK since the early 1600s. These were clubs normally attached to a certain public house where men could join and pay a subscription, the money in the box eventually being used to pay for a member's funeral. They became more popular, and during the later eighteenth century there emerged many 'friendly societies' as they became known, leading the government of the day to regulate them through the Rose Act of 1793. However, as most had developed a fraternal side to their activities and because the government of the time was concerned about societies that met privately (given the events leading to the French Revolution in 1789), other acts of parliament soon followed, namely the Unlawful Oaths Act of 1797, and the Unlawful Societies Act and Combination Acts of 1799. Many of these societies suffered as a result, and had no alternative but to alter their rules and ritual to avoid being prosecuted. These friendly societies grew and developed throughout the nineteenth century despite the rather oppressive legislation, and other Acts, such as the Friendly Society Act of 1875, underlined how important these societies were to working class communities.

Despite the sometimes heavy-handed legislation, the membership of friendly societies boomed in the UK and, as David T. Beito points out in his book *From Mutual Aid to the Welfare State*, membership grew from 600,000 in 1793 to 4 million in 1874.[1] The reason for this growth is simple: friendly societies provided a vital need for the working-class communities in which a 'proper send-off' (i.e. a decent burial) was deemed essential, as the community considered anything less to be disrespectful, a pauper's burial being seen as a disgrace.[2] Sickness benefit was also offered, and the fraternal side of these societies also appealed.

This work aims to discuss these many fraternal societies and their similarities to Freemasonry in terms of the rituals they used, the symbolism they displayed, and

---

1   David T. Beito, *From Mutual Aid to the Welfare State: Fraternal Societies and Social Services 1890-1967*, (North Carolina Press, 2000), p. 7.

2   E.J. Evans, *The Forging of the Modern State: Early Industrial Britain 1783-1870*, (London: Longmans, 1992), p. 151.

the way they assisted their communities through charity and mutual assistance. In doing so the book will examine not only the larger of these 'self-help' societies, such as the Oddfellows, Buffaloes, Druids and Rechabites, but also the lesser-known and more localised societies, such as the Free Gardeners and the Society of the Horseman's Word in Scotland and, in East Anglia, the mysterious Ancient Order of Bonesmen and the Toadsmen.

These societies seemed to have attracted the working men of the period from both industrial and agricultural areas, bonding them together in a recognised (or, in some cases, unrecognised) body that offered them some form of financial protection during an uncertain time of rapid social and economic change. In doing so, working men gained a sense of security and joined a wider circle of like-minded men (and, sometimes, women), a circle that, as we shall see, intermingled with the local community and provided a sense of belonging and togetherness through initiation and secret symbolism.

The work will also analyse the fate of these societies: how some of them split from the original body or amalgamated with other friendly societies and trade unions, and how some of them disappeared completely, leaving mere traces on the once-industrial landscape. This book aims to show that these fraternal societies were an important part of our social history, and that during the industrial period some were as popular as Freemasonry. Their transformation will also be discussed: how the friendly societies were shaped by political tampering, and how the introduction of the welfare state sealed their fate forever.

In contrast, the gentlemen's clubs of the same period are also discussed to present a comparison of the different social needs of the nineteenth and early twentieth centuries, reflecting the stark class differences mirrored in the clubs and societies of the time. These gentlemen's clubs served to provide business contacts and could be used to further a gentleman's career, but they also provided a sense of belonging, some members being known to declare their membership of a certain club with pride.

FREEMASONRY AND WORKING MEN[1]

Masonic lodges in certain industrial towns in the north-west of England attracted an influx of working men during the early nineteenth century, with various lodges – such as the Lodge of Lights in Warrington, a town known for its cotton mills and wire-weaving, and the Lodge of Friendship in Oldham, another cotton town – both providing evidence of working men and labouring tradesmen entering the lodges during this period.

Many of the labouring tradesmen who had joined the Lodge of Lights in the early decades of the nineteenth century had joined from other lodges, such as cotton manufacturer James Knott and weaver Richard Pearson, who had entered the Lodge of Lights from Lodge No. 279 in 1810. In 1820, weaver Henry Harrison and fustian-cutter John Latham both joined the lodge as 'joining members'. Another weaver, William Halton, entered as a joining member from Lodge No. 120 in 1829, and machine-maker Robert Hughes entered as a joining member in 1820. Charles Wainwright, a dyer from Manchester, may have been a member of a lodge under the independent Grand Lodge of Wigan: his grave – adorned with an array of Masonic symbols – can now be found near various other Masonic gravestones at the Parish Church in Warrington.[2]

Besides the labouring tradesmen joining from other lodges there were soldiers who also entered as joining members from other lodges, along with men of more professional occupations, such as excise officers and schoolmasters.[3] Local lodges were certainly not

---

1   Part of this chapter has previously appeared in David Harrison, *The Transformation of Freemasonry*, (Bury St. Edmunds: Arima Publishing, 2010), pp. 37-58. See also David Harrison and John Belton, 'Society in Flux' in *The Journal for the Centre of Research into Freemasonry and Fraternalism*, Vol. 3, (University of Sheffield, 2010).

2   1841 Census for Worsley, Manchester Library, ref: HO107/543/13 and 1851 Census for Levenshulme, Manchester Library, ref: HO107/2219. The Masonic gravestone of Charles Wainwright is located in the churchyard of St. Elphin's, Warrington, a photograph of which can be seen in David Harrison, *The Genesis of Freemasonry*, (Hersham: Lewis Masonic, 2009).

3   *List of Members of the Lodge of Lights, No.148, Masonic Hall, Warrington, 1800-1850*. Not listed.

isolated, and were aware of and in regular contact with other lodges in other towns, Freemasonry being used as an excellent social networking system, which enabled members to visit and join other lodges in other areas. This relationship between lodges created a larger social interaction, and workers and professionals alike could move around the country, settle where the work was, and freely join another lodge, making new social and business contacts in the process. This social nexus was also apparent in the friendly societies and trade unions, allowing workers to join other 'lodges', 'courts', 'tents' or branches if they moved location, automatically giving them social connections.

The benevolent features of joining a Masonic lodge were still apparent during this period. For example, the Masonic Benefit Society attracted a number of members from the Lodge of Lights in 1799,[4] and there seems to have been a relationship between the lodge and the White Hart Benefit Society, members of which were present at the funeral of a certain Brother Johnson in 1802.[5] In February 1802, a collection was made in the lodge on behalf of a certain Brother George Phillips, who was a prisoner for debt in Lancaster Castle.[6] Though a Mason, he was not a member of the Lodge of Lights, but he was obviously seen as a brother in need of help. A similar case featured in the minutes of the lodge in 1812, when Brother Charles Tatlock, a Mason from a Leigh-based lodge, who was also a prisoner in Lancaster Castle, had an application for relief made on his behalf.[7] Charity for a distressed brother featured again in 1805, when Brother Glazebrook applied to Grand Lodge for relief for Brother James Fletcher, who subsequently received the princely sum of £5.[8] The cultivation of self-help during this period would certainly have made Freemasonry appealing, and there is ample evidence that the lodges studied here had beneficent and benevolent features. This view has been developed in recent years within the study of Freemasonry, an organisation that can therefore '*be set firmly alongside friendly societies and other voluntary benevolent organisations in promoting principles of collaboration between self-determining citizens in pursuit of specific goals and interests*'.[9]

---

4   *Minutes of the Lodge of Lights, No.148, Masonic Hall, Warrington, August, 1799.* Not listed.
5   Ibid., *26 January 1802.*
6   Ibid., *22 February 1802.*
7   Ibid., *25 May 1812.*
8   Ibid., *25 November 1805.*
9   See Roger Burt, 'Fraternity and Business Networking in the British Non-ferrous Metal Mining Industry in the Eighteenth and Nineteenth Centuries', (University of Exeter), p. 13, referencing John Money quoting Margaret Jacob in, 'The Masonic Moment: Or Ritual, Replica and Credit: John Wilkes, the Macaroni Parson, and the Making of the Middle Class Mind', *Journal of British Studies*, 32 (1993), p. 372. Also see Roger Burt, 'Industrial Relations In The British Non-Ferrous Mining Industry in the Nineteenth Century', in *Labour History Review*, Vol. 71, No. 1, (April 2006), pp. 57-79.

The Lodge of Friendship in Oldham in Lancashire had, like the Lodge of Lights in Warrington, a list of initiates that included weavers, joiners, turners, blacksmiths and cordwainers, all dominating the lodge during the period 1789-1840. There are also claims for relief mentioned in the minutes, such as in 1792 when a Brother was granted 5s. on the grounds that his wife had been ill for some time, and in 1804 when a gift of 10s. 6d. was given to Brothers who were prisoners in Lancaster Castle. Relief of 6s. was also given to three sailors in 1810, and in 1852 a large sum of £40 was given to victims of a burst reservoir at Holmfirth, with an additional £5 given to the victims of a local boiler explosion. A coffin was purchased by the lodge for the burial of a deceased brother in 1816, and a Benevolent Society was started in connection with the lodge in 1828, with a Sick Fund being founded the following year.[10]

Other industrial towns in Cheshire also had Masonic lodges, which witnessed an influx of labouring tradesmen as members from the 1790s to the 1840s. Strong evidence for labouring tradesmen joining Freemasonry appears in a lodge in the industrial town of Nantwich, which had the rather loyal name of the King's Friends Lodge. In 1808, the minutes reveal that a number of the Brethren of the lodge were of a lesser '*social standing*', being described as '*artizans*', having occupations such as joiner, gardener, locksmith, haymaker, cordwainer, ropemaker, skinner and miller.[11] A Lodge called 'Beneficent' opened in 1789 in Macclesfield, and a Lodge of 'Benevolence' was founded in Stockport, which had originally started as an Antients lodge in 1759. This Lodge of Benevolence also had brethren from mixed social backgrounds, and provides evidence of claims for relief, such as in 1774 when the lodge paid for the burial of two deceased brethren. One particularly interesting claim for relief on 7 February 1774 concerned a travelling Mason who appeared to be commuting from lodge to lodge, perhaps searching for work:

> '*Agreed to give a distress'd Bro. that applies for Relief 1d. per mile, if on horseback 2d. per mile for every mile he goes to another Lodge*'.[12]

---

10   *Minutes of the Lodge of Friendship, No.277, Masonic Hall, Oldham, 1789-1852.* Not listed.

11   Extracts of the Minutes of the Kings Friend's Lodge No. 293, Nantwich, 1798-1831, copied in John Armstrong, *A History of Freemasonry in* Cheshire, (London: Kenning, 1901), pp. 315-322.

12   Ibid. *Extracts from the Lodge of Benevolence No. 83, Stockport,* pp. 282-4.

A lodge in Knutsford, called the Lodge of Harmony, was founded in 1818, many of the founders being members of the Lodge of Lights.[13] William Evans, who was Worshipful Master of the Lodge of Lights at the time, gave a lecture to the Knutsford lodge in 1821,[14] providing evidence of a continuing close relationship between the two lodges. The Knutsford lodge was, however, quite short-lived and was closed in 1839 due to declining attendance.[15] A note after the minutes of the last meeting written by the last Worshipful Master of the lodge, Brother Peter Richardson, reads:

> 'The rich in and about Knutsford take little notice of Freemasonry, the industrious and middle classes very naturally enquire what benefit is there in joining, when explained, they join other societies where they are insured a direct benefit.....if something of this kind was established (a weekly payment in case of sickness and funeral expenses in case of death) in connection with this Lodge it would flourish'.[16]

Richardson obviously had concerns that '*other societies*' were taking potential members away from the lodge, and his final words that closed the minute book clearly testify how these other societies that '*insured a direct benefit*' were attracting certain kinds of men.

Freemasonry, Friendly Societies and Clubs in Public Processions

The Freemasons of the Premier Grand Lodge of England had conducted processions through the streets of London from 1723, when an elegant carriage-parade was held, with the Grand Master Elect being escorted by distinguished Masons dressed in full regalia. However, this was discontinued in 1745, as mock processions were being organised in imitation of the pomp and ceremony.[17] In the north of England however the independent York Grand Lodge had continued with processions at various times,

---

13 *Extracts of the Minutes of the Lodge of Harmony, No.705, Knutsford, 1818-1839*, copied in Armstrong, *History of Freemasonry in Cheshire*, pp. 339-344.

14 Ibid.

15 Ibid.

16 Ibid. A photograph of the Masonic gravestone of Peter Richardson appears in Harrison, *Genesis of Freemasonry*.

17 See David Harrison, *A Quick Guide to Freemasonry*, (Hersham: Lewis Masonic, 2013), p. 52. See also Fred Lomax, *Fred's Five Minute Talks*, (Hersham: Lewis Masonic, 2012).

such as in 1770 when a procession took place through York to celebrate the installation of Sir Thomas Gascoigne as Grand Master on the Feast of St John, and to celebrate the opening of the Druidical Lodge in Rotherham in 1778.[18]

Despite the policy of the Premier or Modern Grand Lodge discouraging public processions, 'regular' Freemasonry began to be much more open again during the early years of the nineteenth century; indeed, as the preceding century closed, in October 1797 in Sheffield, Yorkshire, the local Freemasons were involved in a public procession along with local clubs and other fraternal societies to celebrate the opening of the General Infirmary. A poster advertising the occasion reveals a long list of local clubs, all of which have now disappeared apart from Freemasonry – clubs as obscure as the Revolution Society, who were bizarrely placed next on the list to the Young Royal Society. This diverse group of clubs came together specifically for a day of celebration. Other clubs mentioned on the poster include the Half-Boot Society, the Old Gentlemen's Club, the Bishop Blaze Club and the Grinders' Society. This Grand Procession, as it was called on the poster, does suggest that the Freemasons were still interacting with many local clubs and societies – at least on a social level.

The Poster –The Grand Procession in Sheffield – Wednesday 4 October 1797

From St. Paul's Church to the General Infirmary

This poster clearly shows the relationship between Freemasonry and the civic authorities and the other friendly societies in Sheffield at the time, and it also shows the pre-eminence of Freemasonry as a fraternal society. The procession was divided into three sections.

The first consisted of the various lodges of Freemasons.

The second or central section consisted of the Clerk of Works, Secretary and Architect, The Committee, Medical Gentlemen of the Infirmary, Clergy in their gowns, Trustees of the Charity, Magistrates and Constables.

Poster showing the Grand Procession through Sheffield by various clubs and societies, led by '*the different Lodges of Free masons*', dated to 4 October 1797.

(Courtesy of Sheffield Masonic Hall, Tapton Hall, Sheffield).

---

18 See David Harrison, *The York Grand Lodge*, (Bury St Edmunds: Arima Publishing, 2014), p. 67 and p. 70.

The third division consisted of the Masters, Wardens, Assistants and 'members of those most useful Institutions, the Benefited Societies, or Sick Clubs as they are commonly called'.

In the Masonic procession, in which the Craft is well represented, there are also Royal Arch Masons and Knights Templar. The Royal Brunswick Lodge is named, as is Britannia Lodge; in fact, a total of seven Masonic lodges are mentioned on the poster as taking part, but the other five are not referred to by name.

What is remarkable about this poster is that it reveals the date of the establishment of all of the benefit societies, indeed the first one, The Tailor's Society, dated from 1720, only three years after the formation of the first Masonic Grand Lodge in 1717, while the last one, the Loyal Independent Volunteer Sick Club, dated from 1794.

These were, as is stated, benefit societies or 'box clubs', and they may or may not have had a fraternal side to their organisation. Some have survived to this day, such as the Cutlers and the Foresters. The Shepherd's Society, which was fourth on the list, is now a Friendly Society, but most would have been small local associations and have long since met their demise. Several have curious names, as can be seen from the table below.

The Grand Procession must have been a spectacular sight and have taken a considerable amount of organisation considering the huge numbers of people involved. Indeed, on the poster it states, 'Besides the above, others are expected to join the Procession, whose names have been omitted to be sent in soon enough for publication'.

LIST OF CLUBS AND SOCIETIES IN THE SHEFFIELD GRAND PROCESSION OF 1797		
The Tailor's Society	United Society	Half-boot Society
The Filesmith Society	Reformed Society	Mason's Society
Cutlers Society	Laurel United Society	Waterman's Society
Shepherd's Society	Providence Society	Benevolent Society of Tradesmen & Co.
Old Unanimous Society	Friendly Society	Friendly and United Society
Union Society	Careful Society	Royal Union Society
Carpenters Sick Society	Young Men's Sick Society	Rodney Club
Society Depending on Providence	Green Forester's Society	Young Royal Society
Grinder's Society	Tradesmen's Society	Revolution Society
Bishop Blaze Club	Tradesmen Society	Prince of Wales Society
Old Gentlemen's Club	Brazier's Society	Scissorsmith Society
Indefatigable Union	Young Society	Loyal Independent Volunteer Sick Club

The poster was sold at a price of one penny each and, after the procession, a Dinner was served for those who wished to partake of it at the Angel Inn for seven shillings and sixpence, Ordinary and Extraordinary.

In Halifax, Yorkshire, in October 1809, there was a procession to celebrate the Jubilee of George III, which not only included a number of Masonic lodges from around Halifax and Bradford but also the local militia and the '*Original Lodge of Odd Fellows (No. 6)*'. All lodges paraded to the church, where a sermon was given, and then the Masons gathered for a meal. A house-to-house collection was also conducted to give food, drink and clothing to the poor, and £42 10s. was given by the Masonic lodges to the Halifax General Dispensary. The local lodges themselves had decided to take part in what could be seen as a show of patriotism in the industrial town, and had openly co-operated with other local groups and societies, the '*Odd Fellows*' getting a particular mention in the minutes of the Lodge of Probity, one of the Masonic lodges that took part.[19]

Over the border in Lancashire the Lodge of Lights participated in many public events, one such being a procession by all the Warrington clubs celebrating the coronation of George IV in July 1821. The minutes of the lodge describe a lively meeting held before the procession[20], and a local poster from the period, now on public display in Warrington Parish Church, lists the local Freemasons leading a march of nineteen local clubs through the streets of the town. These clubs included many friendly societies and trade clubs, such as the Union Club, the Union Coffee House Club and the Subscription Club, all representing their respective taverns and coffee-houses. Another well-established society, the Amicable Club, also made an appearance. Local trades were also represented, such as the spinners, pin-makers, tin-plate workers and glass makers, all marching behind the Freemasons – symbolising perhaps the hierarchy of the societies in the town.[21]

Though the Lodge of Lights celebrated the coronation of George IV, it did not proceed with a proposed procession for the coronation of William IV ten years later, probably as a result of the poor attendance and the small number of members that the lodge had during 1831. Other clubs and societies did however take part in a procession in Warrington to

---

19 T.W. Hanson, *The Lodge of Probity No. 61: 1738-1938*, (Halifax: The Lodge of Probity, 1938), p. 184.
20 *Minutes of the Lodge of Lights, No.148, Masonic Hall, Warrington, 19 July 1821*. Not listed.
21 See the photograph of the poster advertising the Coronation procession of George IV in July 1821, held in St. Elphin's Church, Warrington.

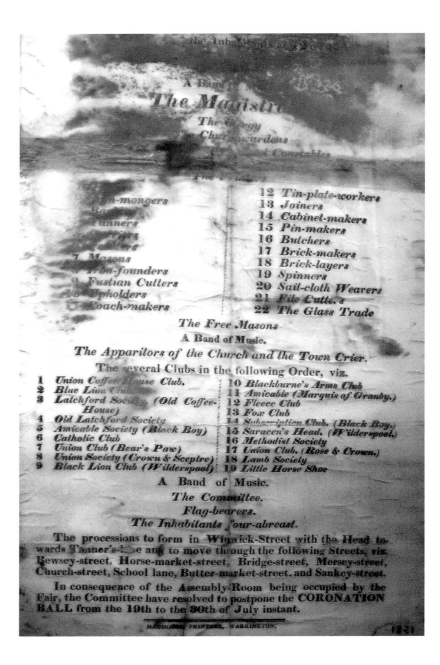

the Inhabitants of

A Band

The Magistr

The Clergy
Church-wardens
Constables

12 Tin-plate-workers
13 Joiners
14 Cabinet-makers
15 Pin-makers
16 Butchers
17 Brick-makers
18 Brick-layers
19 Spinners
20 Sail-cloth Wearers
21 File Cutters
22 The Glass Trade

n-mongers

anners

7 Masons
8 Iron-founders
9 Fustian Cutters
10 pholders
11 Coach-makers

The Free Masons
A Band of Music.
The Apparitors of the Church and the Town Crier.
The several Clubs in the following Order, viz.

1 Union Coffee House Club.
2 Blue Lion Club
3 Latchford Society (Old Coffee-House)
4 Old Latchford Society
5 Amicable Society (Black Boy)
6 Catholic Club
7 Union Club (Bear's Paw)
8 Union Society (Crown & Sceptre)
9 Black Lion Club (Wilderspool)
10 Blackburne's Arms Club
11 Amicable (Marquis of Granby.)
12 Fleece Club
13 Fox Club
14 Subscription Club. (Black Boy.)
15 Saracen's Head. (Wilderspool.)
16 Methodist Society
17 Union Club. (Rose & Crown.)
18 Lamb Society
19 Little Horse Shoe

A Band of Music.
The Committee.
Flag-bearers.
The Inhabitants four-abreast.

The processions to form in Winwick-Street with the Head towards Tanner's-lane and to move through the following Streets, viz. Bewsey-street, Horse-market-street, Bridge-street, Mersey-street, Church-street, School lane, Butter-market-street, and Sankey-street.

In consequence of the Assembly-Room being occupied by the Fair, the Committee have resolved to postpone the CORONATION BALL from the 19th to the 30th of July instant.

HADDOCK, PRINTERS, WARRINGTON.

1821

celebrate the coronation, the Oddfellows taking a prominent role.[22] A procession by Freemasons also took place in Manchester in honour of the new King, with lodges from Liverpool also taking part, as well as the 'Union of Odd Fellows' and the 'Royal Foresters'.[23]

In Wigan, a neighbouring industrial town, the Wigan Grand Lodge celebrated the coronation of Victoria in June 1838, parading through Wigan in regalia with the banner of the Grand Lodge. The Wigan Grand Lodge was an independent Grand Lodge of Freemasons, which had a number of local lodges under its sway. Centred as it was in a

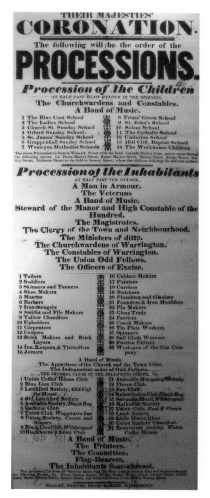

LEFT: Poster showing a procession through Warrington, Lancashire, with the '*Free Masons*' leading the various local clubs and societies to celebrate the coronation of George IV in July 1821. (*Photograph by David Harrison. Courtesy of St Elphin's Church*)

RIGHT: Poster showing a procession through Warrington ten years later to celebrate the coronation of William IV, though this time the various local clubs and societies are led by the '*Independent Order of Odd Fellows*'. (*Photograph by David Harrison. Courtesy of St Elphin's Church*)

---

22 *Minutes of the Lodge of Lights, No.148, Masonic Hall, Warrington, 1831.* Also see the photograph advertising the Coronation procession of William IV, held in St. Elphin's Church, Warrington.

23 Anon., *The History of The Lodge of Harmony No. 220*, (Liverpool, 1948), p. 9. See also Andy Durr, 'Chicken and Egg – the Emblem Book and Freemasonry: the Visual and Material Culture of Associated Life', in *AQC*, Vol. 118, (2006), pp. 20-36, in which Durr discusses the procession to celebrate the coronation of William IV in Manchester, and how the various Associations involved (Freemasonry, the Oddfellows and various Trade Societies) used similar styles of regalia and used similar symbolism and iconography on their banners, certificates and commemorative jugs.

heavily industrial area and having a large number of working men as members, a sickness and burial fund was naturally established, the subscription fees being increased at various times in accordance with the condition of the funds. After a period of debt the Wigan Grand Lodge began to manage the funds better, and by 1878 they were actually able to lend Wigan Corporation £200 for five years at 4 per cent interest, the interest later being used to establish a contingent fund to assist needy and distressed brethren. In this respect the Wigan Grand Lodge was operating on a similar basis to the Oddfellows, Foresters and Druids by maintaining the character of a benevolent society.[24]

On 22 December 1836, the Lodge of Lights held a lavish ceremony for the laying of the keystone of a new bridge over the Mersey, leaving a number of offerings, including a Masonic glass box, showing the set-square and compass, and a number of coins. The son of the architect of the bridge, George Gamon of Knutsford, was made a Freemason especially to enable him to participate in the ceremony. A procession had taken place from the Market Hall to the bridge, in which boys from the Bluecoat School also took part, along with local Constables and Churchwardens. Money was collected to give the Bluecoat boys a meal, and other Lancashire lodges attended the ceremony, such as the Lodge of Harmony from Liverpool.[25] Freemasonry was definitely becoming more 'people-friendly', especially in the industrial towns of the north, and was trying to become more open to society. An effort to be less secretive and more public, to get involved with local charities and education, and to build up a relationship with the authorities and the local gentry all played a part in this. By taking part in marches and public celebrations, Freemasonry was promoting itself in their particular town, and in this way attempted to attract new members. The benevolent aspects of Freemasonry were still apparent in the lodge: in 1831, for example, the lodge paid out 8s. 10d. for relief, and petitions were quite common, being put forward on a regular basis during this period.[26] In 1845, there were several petitions for relief by the brethren,[27] yet by the late 1840s changes began to appear in the lodge make-up, and claims for relief became rare.

---

24 See David Harrison, *The Liverpool Masonic Rebellion and the Wigan Grand Lodge*, (Bury St. Edmunds: Arima Publishing, 2012), p. 70.

25 *Minutes of the Lodge of Lights, No.148, Masonic Hall, Warrington, 22 December 1836.* Not listed. The items are now on display at the Warrington Museum. See also Anon., *The History of The Lodge of Harmony No. 220*, (Liverpool, 1948), p.9.

26 *Minutes of the Lodge of Lights, No.148, Masonic Hall, Warrington, August, 1831.* Not Listed.

27 Ibid., *1845.*

The Transformation of Freemasonry

Perhaps because of the rise of the Oddfellows and Foresters in Warrington[28] or possibly because of trade union developments, the Lodge of Lights had fewer and fewer labouring tradesmen joining by the 1840s.[29] More industrialists joined the lodge, such as the charismatic Sir Gilbert Greenall, a local brewer who, when he joined in 1850, was the Conservative MP for Warrington.[30] Shaw Thewlis, a local file manufacturer, joined in 1846, and many other professional gentlemen entered the lodge, such as local surgeon William Hunt, solicitor James Bayley, and James Jones the Deputy Constable.[31] The Warrington Academy, which had links to local Freemasons and had closed in 1786, was still very much remembered, and the charitable ethos of Freemasonry filtered into the more philanthropic ideals of the industrialists and professionals of Warrington.

The local industrialists re-shaped the town, becoming involved in local politics and gradual social reform. Many of these factory-owners, such as the Stubs, Rylands and Greenall families, became involved in local Freemasonry,[32] and they also played a major role in the learned societies that evolved in the nineteenth century. They helped to maintain the Masonic ethos of education by supporting the establishment of civic centres such as the Warrington Library and Museum, the Art College, and the School of Science, echoing the involvement of early Masons such as Benjamin Yoxall in local educational pursuits. Many of the learned societies supported by local Freemasons, such as the Mechanics Institute, met in the old Academy buildings, and the members of the Lodge of Lights were present during the ceremony for the laying of the foundation-stone for the Library and Museum in 1855.

Many other local Freemasons became involved in these local learned societies, such as George Hughes and Thomas Morris, both Curators of the Natural History Society.[33] Two of the pioneers of the society were Peter Rylands and Joseph Stubs, both local

28 *Oddfellows Contribution Book, Loyal Orange Lodge, No.143, 1835-42*, Warrington Library, reference MS280 & *Foresters Laws & Regulations, Warrington, 1842*, Warrington Library, reference p1423.

29 *List of Members of the Lodge of Lights, No.148, Masonic Hall, Warrington, 1840-1850*. Not listed.

30 Ibid., *28 June 1850*.

31 Ibid., *1837-1850*. Also see *Warrington Trade Directories, 1792-1855*, Warrington Library, reference S10121.

32 *List of Members of the Lodge of Lights, No.148, Masonic Hall, Warrington, 1837-1865*. Not listed.

33 Ibid., *1837-1865*. Also see *Minutes of General Meetings of the Natural History Society, 1837-53*, Warrington Library, reference MS22.

industrialists and members of the Lodge of Lights.[34] Stubs extended his involvement in local charity by serving on the committee for the Warrington Dispensary and Infirmary. The local Unitarian Chapel had held Sunday School classes since the early 1800s, and had been involved in welfare work, forming a sick club and a clothing club. In 1862, the local Unitarian Minister, J. Nixon Porter, became a Freemason and continued a link between the Lodge of Lights and the Unitarian Ministry which had started with John Seddon, the founder of the Academy.[35]

In Yorkshire the Royal Yorkshire Lodge in Keighley, which had also witnessed many labouring tradesmen enter the lodge from the 1790s, also began to have an increased influx of professionals, industrialists, and businessmen (including men from the 'High Street', such as butchers and grocers) after the 1840s. Labouring tradesmen appeared less and less, and by the 1840s, the transformation of the membership is evident, with the lodge being filled with local gentlemen, schoolmasters and manufacturers.[36]

Why did this change take place? The social historian Eric J. Evans, in his book *The Forging of the Modern State*, has argued that a greater divide between the working classes and middle classes occurred after the Reform Act of 1832, the old collaborations between these middle and working classes disintegrating after what he termed the '*middle class betrayal of 1832*'. Evans also claims that in the industrial cotton-mill towns of Lancashire there was a '*greater distance observed between the master and the spinner*'.[37] As class-consciousness developed, Freemasonry became increasingly attractive to professionals, businessmen and industrialists, while the working men who had shared the lodges with them in various industrial towns in the first half of the nineteenth century began to look elsewhere, joining other clubs and societies. The now better-organised and legal trade unions[38] and the increasingly popular 'ritualistic'

---

34   Ibid.
35   *List of Members of the Lodge of Lights, No.148, Masonic Hall, Warrington, 28 July 1862.* Not listed.
36   *List of Members of the Royal Yorkshire Lodge No. 265* in J. Ramsden Riley, *The History of the Royal Yorkshire Lodge*, (Yorkshire, 1889), pp. 79-87.
37   Evans, *Forging of the Modern State*, pp. 172-173.
38   The Combination Acts were finally repealed in 1824, but an amended Combination Act was passed the following year, which permitted trade unions but restricted their activity. Secret oath-taking was still causing concern to the authorities. Despite the Tolpuddle Martyrs and the collapse of Robert Owen's 'Grand National Consolidated Trades Union' in 1834, the more organised skilled-trades unions flourished, such as the 'Old Mechanics' and the 'Amalgamated Society of Carpenters and Joiners'. In 1867 a Royal Commission on Trade Unions was established, which eventually led to the Trade Union Act of 1871 which secured the legal status of Trade Unions and protected their funds.

friendly societies such as the Oddfellows, Druids, Foresters and the IOR – which from about 1841 had started to introduce medical benefits[39] – attracted more working men, and this development coincides exactly with the time when Masonic lodges in the industrial towns featured fewer and fewer labouring tradesmen and factory workers in their make-up.

The benevolent values of Freemasonry were evident throughout the late eighteenth and early nineteenth centuries, with support being given to the widows and children of deceased brethren, funerals being taken care of, and relief being provided for members who were in debt. This would make joining a lodge a very attractive proposition for a labouring tradesman, and would be extremely advantageous to his family, especially when one considers that 'a good send-off' was important in working-class culture. The numbers of labouring men that entered local lodges became fewer and, as we shall see, this shift coincided with the development of more organised legal trade unions, and especially with the development of friendly societies. The introduction of more organised Burial Societies, such as the 'Liverpool Independent Legal Victoria Burial Society' founded in 1843,[40] and benefit societies like the 'Benefit Building Society' established in Liverpool in 1865, would also have specifically attracted the working classes who were interested in burial cover.[41] Freemasonry seems to have become more elitist as more local industrialists, businessmen and professionals joined, but support for local charity and education was still as strong as ever as local lodges continued to support their communities. As will be discussed later, the many gentlemen's clubs also offered the middle and upper classes of England access to networking and a social scene of pleasure-seeking, far removed from the deprivation of the working-class areas and the hardships of the industrial communities.

---

39 Jack S. Blocker, David M. Fahey, and Ian R. Tyrrell, *Alcohol and Temperance in Modern History*, (ABC-CLIO Ltd., 2003), p. 513.

40 The Liverpool Independent Legal Victoria Burial Society, founded in 1843 in Liverpool, charged a premium of ½d. or 1d. per week to cover funeral costs. It became known as the Liverpool Victoria Friendly Society in 1893.

41 *Rules of The Clarence Street Permanent Benefit Building Society, Established at Liverpool, 3 May 1865*, (Liverpool: Thomas Walmsley, 1868). Countless 'Assurance' and 'Benefit' companies were founded at this time, all targeting the 'working classes', for example, in *The Warrington Guardian, Saturday 9 April 1853*, the front page was mainly taken up with adverts for Assurance companies such as 'The Tines Life Assurance and Guarantee Company' and 'The English Widows Fund and General Life Assurance Association'.

Freemasonry, Trade Unions and Friendly Societies

Trade unions and friendly societies may have eventually tempted the labouring tradesmen away from Freemasonry – especially lodges in the industrial areas of northern England – as the friendly societies and unions offered various benefits for sickness and burial as well as support during industrial action. Many friendly societies like the Oddfellows also met in lodges, and used very similar regalia and displayed similar symbolism to Freemasonry, from the banners and marches of trade unions to the aprons, jewels and sashes of the Buffaloes. Ritual had also played a large part in the early development of the Oddfellows, Foresters and Druids and, as we shall see in more depth later on, balloting was used and oaths were taken. There was certainly a relationship between Freemasonry and friendly societies such as the Oddfellows, with members freely joining both and enjoying the benefit of dual membership.[42] The Oddfellows, like Freemasonry, built Halls for lodge meetings, such as the elegant Oddfellows Hall in Chester and the Halls studied for the purpose of this work in Halebank and St. Helens.

As a prominent example, the Oddfellows certainly had many elements of Freemasonry in their Order, and in the early decades of the 1800s the Oddfellows kept in close contact with Masonry. For example, an article in the long-running *Oddfellow's Magazine* in 1829 declared how the society was originally instituted on Masonic principles and commented on the moral codes of brotherly love which were strong features of Freemasonry.[43] Another example of this close link was seen when a prospective Oddfellows member was turned down for membership after the society had sought advice from the Masonic Grand Lodge[44]. As we have seen, the Oddfellows had taken part in processions with Freemasons, and there seemed to be a social interaction between Masonry and other clubs during the late eighteenth and early nineteenth centuries. Trade unions also strongly reflected aspects of Masonry, using terms such as 'brother' while adopting secret codes and handshakes, especially in the early part of the nineteenth century when they were forced into the shadows due to legislation. Indeed, some 'unions' had to act in utmost secrecy and could face harsh punishment.

---

42 See P.H.J.H. Gosden, *The Friendly Societies In England 1815-1875*, (Manchester: Manchester University Press, 1961). See also Andrew Prescott, 'The Spirit of Association: Freemasonry and Early Trade Unions', A Paper Presented at the Canonbury Masonic Research Centre, 30 May 2001, in Hibiscus Masonic Review, Vol. I, 2007 ISBN 978-0-59543-054-3.

43 Gosden, *Friendly Societies in England*, p. 127.

44 Ibid., taken from the Minutes and Documents of the Grand Committees of the Manchester Unity of Oddfellows, 15 March 1815.

The Friendly Society of Agricultural Labourers

The Friendly Society Act of 1793 gave friendly societies legal status and protection of their funds and, importantly, a reprieve from the onslaught of the Combination Acts of 1799 and 1800. The legal protection of their funds, used to support working men and their families for sickness and burial, was thought to reduce the demand for poor relief, and the Act of 1793 was an attempt to regulate the many friendly societies that were being founded all over England and Wales.

Because of this, many illegal radical gatherings subsequently adopted the guise of Friendly Societies, with groups of labouring men being driven underground by the Combination Acts to meet in private to discuss their grievances. An example of working men coming together and being persecuted in an effort to protect their rights can be seen with the formation of the 'Friendly Society of Agricultural Labourers' by six Dorset farm labourers in March 1834, otherwise known as the Tolpuddle Martyrs. The Friendly Society of Agricultural Labourers, which was effectively a trade union, was formed to protect the wages of their members. They had an initiation ritual which included the taking of an oath and – reminiscent of the Craft rituals of Freemasonry – the leading of the initiate blindfolded into the 'lodge' room where he was shown a picture of a skeleton. The Tolpuddle Martyrs were arrested for swearing illegal oaths after a complaint from a local landowner, and sentenced to seven years' transportation. After popular protests, all but one were released in 1836, with the last member being freed the following year.

United Machine Workers Association badge from the 1930s.

(Collection of David Harrison)

The Old Mechanics

Another example is the 'Journeymen Steam Engine and Machine Makers Friendly Society' – or 'Old Mechanics' as they were known – which was founded by the Manchester-based John White, who had campaigned ardently for the society and had travelled to industrial towns like Stockport, Oldham and Bolton on Saturday nights to promote it, walking home on a Sunday and changing his lodgings every three or four weeks to avoid the constables. Though, at the beginning, the 'Old Mechanics' used the term 'Friendly Society' in their title, it was evident that they were really a trade union.

When the society was well established White acted as treasurer, and had to hide as much as £6000 up the chimney and in the cellar of his house as trade unions had no legal security for their funds in the banks. The many branches of the society met in local public houses, where the landlord held the box containing the funds, the rules of the society stating that:

> 'the box shall contain three different locks and keys outside also three different locks and keys for the cash drawer which shall be kept by the president and the two acting stewards'.

A photo of a 'three-locked box', used by many friendly societies and clubs, and usually kept by the landlord of the pub where the society met. There were three keys, and the box could only be opened when all three key-holders were present. This particular example was used by the **Sutton Oddfellows Friendly Society**. *(Courtesy of the Rotherham Branch of Oddfellows)*

A print showing an oath-taking ceremony of the 'Old Mechanics' Friendly Society.
(Courtesy of One hundred and fifty years progress, 1811-1961, Amalgamated Engineering Union)

The 'Old Mechanics' had an initiation ceremony with hints of Masonic ritual: behind specially-hung curtains in a room in a public house a new member would receive a password and be required to swear secrecy on the Bible. A pistol was pointed at him while he took his oath and a skull was revealed to him to remind him of what would become of him if he revealed the society's secrets.[45]

The 'Old Mechanics' became very successful due to their secrecy and also thanks to their uniting of the old and new classes of workmen: for example, by bringing the older millwrights and the newer engineers together, and changing and adapting by amalgamating numerous societies to become a stronger 'union'. By 1851 the 'Old Mechanics' and the newly-amalgamated societies called themselves the 'Amalgamated

---

45   P.W. Kingsford, *Engineers, Inventors and Workers*, (London: Edward Arnold, 1973), pp. 88-90.

An apron for the Loyal United Free Mechanics, showing various symbols that are also found in Freemasonry, such as the All-seeing Eye, the Sun and the Moon, the Skull and Crossed Bones, the Coffin, the Beehive, the Ark, and the compass and square (albeit reversed).

(Courtesy of Tapton Hall, Sheffield)

Society of Engineers, Machinists, Smiths, Millwrights and Patternmakers', and by the end of the year had 10,841 members, with a new trade protection fund to provide strike pay, and the ability to provide benefits for unemployment, sickness, pension, accidents and funerals, all for 1s. per week.[46]

Co-operative Societies

The many co-operative societies that emerged used an array of popular symbols to represent unity, industry and strength, which were similar to some Masonic symbolism and to those used by friendly societies and trade unions. One of these symbols was the

The shaking of hands was a powerful symbol, with obvious Masonic overtones, and was adopted by the Co-op, as seen on this nineteenth-century building in Tuebrook, Liverpool. *(Photograph by David Harrison)*

46 Ibid.

beehive, which represents industry and the idea that if people work together for the same goal then it can be achieved: one bee alone cannot survive, but with others working industriously in a beehive it thrives to produce life-giving honey. Some co-operative societies even used bees in their names, an example being the Daisyfield Industrial Bees Co-operative Society. The beehive symbol was also used by the Provident Mutual Life Assurance, originally founded in 1840. Another symbol used by certain co-operative societies was the shaking of hands, also found in Freemasonry: it represents friendship, loyalty and brotherly love. This symbol can be seen on the Victorian Co-Op building in West Derby Road, Tuebrook, Liverpool.

Other co-operative symbols include the rainbow flag, which was adopted by the International Co-Operative Alliance in 1925 and which represents unity in diversity, the seven different colours having seven different meanings. The rainbow also symbolises the Enlighten-ment and progress. The wheat sheaf is another symbol which frequently occurs in the symbolism of other friendly societies, and represents unity and plenty; again, like the beehive, it represents how working together can result in a plentiful harvest. The symbol of the rowing-boat has also been used by various trade unions, such as the 'Old Mechanics', and signifies that a boat can be used purposefully if the rowers work together, pulling in the same direction, otherwise the boat will be directionless and useless.

Other Smaller Societies

The main friendly societies such as the Oddfellows and Foresters were, however, not the only option, and smaller and more intimate clubs and societies sprang up in various towns across the country, meeting in local pubs and church halls. In fact, there were so many it is impossible to list them all, but an example from Leigh in Lancashire was the New Union Society, which met at the Boar's Head in Pennington.

In its rules and orders for the governance of the society it claimed that it had been founded on 5 November 1789 although, despite its age, it was quite a small club and appears to have been restricted to younger members aged between 18 and 30. The Officers listed were one Clerk, Treasurer, one Inspector, one High Constable and three Stewards. New members must not have suffered from any disability or infirmity and, at the quarterly meetings, members would be expected to pay a 2s. fee, i.e. 1s. 9d. for the 'box' and 3d. for liquor. New members had to pay for two full years before any entitlement could be claimed.[47]

---

47 Miscellaneous newspaper reports, Pennington, Leigh. Leigh Local Studies, WLCT.

A further example of the smaller type of clubs was the Chowbent Five Pound Club which met in a private house. The Leigh Chronicle of 31 May 1873 reports:

> '*The chairman took the meeting and in addressing the members he reminded them of the good that came from such clubs to the different tradesmen in Atherton and stated that the present one would come more within the reach of the working classes and suited more their requirements. He then read over a list of shares, which are upwards of 240; these had increased from 180 in the previous eighteen months. As was common with all the friendly and fraternal societies at the time, they offered a loyal toast to The Queen and The Prince of Wales*'.[48]

From the above it would appear that the Five Pound Club was slightly more upmarket and aimed at tradesmen rather than the ordinary working man; however, from the chairman's statement it would seem that they were perhaps trying to expand into a broader market and to include other members of the working class.

Clubs became a vital part of the male social scene in the eighteenth century, as renowned historian Roy Porter explains in his book *Enlightenment*: '*Given half the chance, English men would set up a club where they could be at ease smoking, talking or indulging themselves in blissful silence*'.[49] London was indeed full of clubs, but there were also a good many located in the provinces: in Warrington there was the Amicable Club, a dining-club that included a number of local prominent industrialists, the minute books revealing a rather large alcohol bill.[50] There was also the patriotic Pitt Club and the Eagle & Child Club, both dining-clubs.[51] In Liverpool there was the Free and Easy Society which, like Freemasonry and various friendly societies, heavily promoted charity. An example of the exuberant generosity of its members can be seen during the anniversary dinner of the society, which was held on 1 January 1817: '*After dinner members will dispose of cash in the Treasurers Funds to Charities they think proper*'.The 'Free and Easy Johns' as they were known, were assembled into lodges, and

---

48   The Leigh Chronicle, 31 May 1873, Leigh Local Studies, WLCT.
49   Roy Porter, *Enlightenment*, (London: Penguin, 2000), p. 440.
50   *Minutes from the Amicable Club, 1788-1803*, Warrington Library, reference MS13.
51   *Minutes from the Eagle & Child Club, 1781-1785*, Warrington Library, reference MS14. See also Harrison, *Transformation of Freemasonry*, p. 31.

can be traced back to the later eighteenth century.[52] There were countless other clubs: Laurence Dermott, in the third edition of *Ahiman Rezon* in 1778, mentions, among others, the Farting Club and the Ugly Faced Club, revealing that some of the clubs *'have, in imitation of the free-masons, called their club by the name of lodge, and their presidents by the title of grand master'.*[53]

These fraternal dining-clubs were also evident across the Pennines, e.g. the York-based Good Humour Club, which operated from c. 1725-1800 and met at Sunton's Coffee House in Coney Street, York. The club merrily celebrated the twin virtues of companionship and conviviality – virtues that were not too dissimilar to the ones found in Freemasonry. The club, which was also known as the Doctor's Club (each member was given the honorary title of Doctor) was one of the many gentlemen's clubs that operated in York during the eighteenth century, and throughout its existence included many local Freemasons from both the York and 'Modern' Grand Lodges.[54]

Beehive symbol for Provident Mutual. *(Photograph by David Harrison)*

---

52 Liverpool Mercury 27 December 1816, issue 289, the Anniversary Dinner was advertised as meeting at the home of James Sweeney of Mersey St. on 1 January 1817. Liverpool Masonic rebel John Eltonhead was President of the Society in 1816; see also Harrison, *Liverpool Masonic Rebellion and the Wigan Grand Lodge*, p. 36.

53 Laurence Dermott, *Ahiman Rezon*, (London: 1778), p. xli. Also see Harrison, *Genesis of Freemasonry* p. 168.

54 See <http://goodhumour.laurencesternetrust.org.uk/history/members-of-the-club/> [accessed 22 August 2013]. Two recently discovered minute books belonging to the Good Humour Club; a minute book dating from 1743, the other dating from 1781, led to research conducted by Hugh Murray for the Laurence Sterne Trust in 2013, leading to an exhibition regarding the history of the club at Shandy Hall during the summer of that year. See also Harrison, *The York Grand Lodge*, p. 131.

THE INDEPENDENT ORDER OF RECHABITES

In Britain during the Industrial Revolution in the 19th century there was a general belief among the middle classes that the excessive consumption of alcohol by working class men was bad for society in general. Whilst the middle and upper classes had their wine with their dinner at home or attended gentlemen's clubs, the working man frequented the local pub, of which there were many, especially after the Beerhouse Act of 1830 in England, which allowed anyone with two guineas to obtain a licence to brew and sell beer. Of course, as social historian Eric J. Evans points out, the pub was probably a lot warmer and cosier than the damp, dark cellar, tenement or terraced house that the working man and his family lived in. The pub was also a place to socialise, and beer was a lot safer to drink than the water in the industrial towns.[1]

The temperance movement in England was initiated mainly by the middle classes with a view to controlling drunkenness, especially among men who worked in the developing industrial towns and cities. It was felt that a man would be better off not spending his money on alcohol, that it was wasteful, and that it was a cause of poverty and crime. There were also the dangerous after-effects of excessive drinking and the potential for injury when using machinery, or of a man turning up late for work, something which employers in the rapidly-changing employment scene would not tolerate.

The Independent Order of Rechabites, or the Sons and Daughters of Rechab, was founded on 25 August 1835 in Salford, near Manchester, England, to provide funeral and sickness benefits to members and as a total-abstinence society with a strict moral code, with membership drawn mainly from the skilled working classes.[2] However, there is a claim that the movement was really started in 1832 by a group of gentlemen referred to as 'the seven men of Preston'. A certain Mr Joseph Livesey, who had a large

---

1 Evans, *Forging of the Modern State*, p. 151.
2 See Jack S. Blocker, David M. Fahey, and Ian R. Tyrrell, *Alcohol and Temperance in Modern History*, (ABC-CLIO Ltd., 2003), p. 513.

provision business and published a monthly journal called the 'Moral Reformer' (which ran from January 1831 to December 1833), began to practise abstinence from fermented liquors. He was led to this course by that passage in the autobiography of Benjamin Franklin (between whose character and Mr Livesey's there were striking points of resemblance) in which he relates his experience as a journeyman printer in London in 1725, when he abstained from ale and tried to convince his fellow-workmen that their favourite beverage was not a strengthening one but one that caused weakness, and that by spending so much of their money on ale they were, as Franklin says, '*Keeping themselves always under*'.[3]

On 22 August a pledge of abstinence from all strong drink, drawn up by Mr Livesey, was signed in his shop by him and by Mr John King, and on 1 September at a meeting in the Cock-Pit, after the new proposals had been discussed, Mr Livesey, having written the pledge, appended the names of those who had given their consent at the time: '*We agree to abstain from all liquors of an intoxicating quality, whether ale, porter, wine, or ardent spirit, except as medicine*'. The seven names as written down by Mr Livesey were in the following order: John Gratrix, Edward Dickinson, John Broadbent, John Smith, Joseph Livesey, David Anderton, and the aforementioned John King.

Around these 'seven men of Preston' there gathered, in the course of time, a legendary and almost mythical status as the founders of the total abstinence cause. The seven names cannot be spoken of as seven signatures since they were all put down in Mr Livesey's handwriting, but they have an honoured place in Temperance history, even though the association of the names was casual and not one of the seven men except Mr Livesey exerted any powerful influence on behalf of the new movement. The influence of these 'seven men' in promoting the cause of abstinence thus inspired the formation of other groups, especially in the industrial north-west of England.[4]

The Salford Unity of Rechabites, founded in 1835 by a small group of abstainers who wanted to form a secret fraternal benefit society, called their first lodge 'Tent Ebenezer, No.1', because the sons of Rechab were apparently instructed by the Almighty not only to abstain from wine but also to live in tents – each Tent being

3   Benjamin Franklin was of course a leading Freemason in North America and was at one time Provincial Grand Master of the Grand Lodge of Pennsylvania in 1734 and in 1755 participated in the dedication of America's first Masonic Hall in Philadelphia; see Mark A. Tabbert, *American Freemasons: Three Centuries of Building Communities*, (New York: New York University Press, 2005), p. 35.

4   Richardson Campbell, *History of the Rechabite Order*, (Published by the Board of Directors of the Order, 1911. Republished by Nabu Public Domain Reprints, USA), pp. 3-4.

OFFENCE	Fine (in shillings and pence)	Rule
TABLE OF FINES from Richardson Campbell, History of the Rechabite Order, (Published by the Board of Directors of the Order, 1911. Republished by Nabu Public Domain Reprints, USA), pp.31-32.		
Guardian admitting a brother without the word	1s. 0d.	3
Guardian leaving the door	10s. 0d.	3
Officers refusing to serve after being elected	1s. 0d.	5
Officers for non-attendance without apology	1s. 0d.	9
Officers, for not being present at eight o'clock	0s. 3d.	9
Members of Committee for non-attendance	0s. 6d.	11
Members for not being present at half-past eight o'clock	0s. 3d.	11
For swearing, &c., each offence	0s. 3d.	12
For reading, &c., during Tent hours, 6d., not less than,	0s. 3d.	12
For disobeying the CR (Chief Ruler) when called to order	0s. 3d.	14
For interrupting a brother when speaking	0s. 1d.	16
For proposing or introducing a person contrary to the laws, One Pound and not less than	10s. 0d.	18
Any brother that divulges a brother's name who voted against any one being admitted a member, or revealing the private affairs to persons not belonging to the Order, One Pound, and not less than	10s. 0d.	20
Guardians, for allowing brothers etc. to leave Tent during singing etc.	0s. 3d.	23
For not rising when addressing the Officers	0s. 1d.	24
For neglecting to address the Officers by their proper title	0s. 1d.	25
For not giving the Counter-sign upon entering and before leaving the Tent	0s. 1d.	26
For a false accusation	5s. 0d.	29
Ditto, second offence	7s. 6d.	29
Brothers misbehaving during Tent hours	1s. 0d.	32
Quarrelling with, or striking a brother	5s. 0d.	32
For breaking the Pledge of Abstinence from all intoxicating liquor	2s. 0d.	41
Ditto, second offence	5s. 0d.	41
Ditto, third offence	10s. 0d.	41
Ditto, fourth offence	20s. 0d.	41
Any brother knowing of a dishonest brother and not informing of him	2s. 0d.	44
Giving the password to an ineffective member	5s. 0d.	48
Brothers attending Tent without sash and not making an apology	0s. 1d.	52
Secretary not being present at eight o'clock	0s. 1d.	56
Secretary omitting to call over the names of the Officers at the proper time	0s. 3d.	56
Secretary, for non-attendance	2s. 6d.	56
Brothers smoking, &c., during making	0s. 3d.	59

given names from the Bible to reflect morality. Soon there were Tents for male adults (over 16) and female adults (over 12); for boys, aged 12-16; and for children of both sexes aged from 5 to 12. All who could write were required to 'sign the pledge' saying (among many other things) that they would '*abstain from all intoxicating liquors except in religious ordinances, or when prescribed by a legally qualified medical practitioner during sickness which renders one incapable of following any employment*'.

The opening of a second 'Tent' called the Good Samaritan Tent soon followed at the Temperance Coffee House of John Holt in Brown Street, Salford, about three months after the opening of the first 'Tent'. At this meeting John Holt proved a very able speaker on the temperance question and a dedicated worker in the movement. Many respectful tributes were paid to him as one of the earliest labourers in the cause of sobriety. For a long time before his death he suffered from heart disease and knew that his end was near. On the evening of his death he lectured at Stalybridge and addressed the rather sombre meeting as a person who was descending to the grave, and hoped his hearers would consider him in that position while he was speaking of the evils of intemperance and the blessings of total abstinence. He spoke for upwards of an hour, then went to his lodgings, had supper, and died that night.

The opening of the Good Samaritan Tent No. 2 suggested that the Order was growing quickly but, as we shall see, the IOR, despite being a society that promoted temperance, did have its critics. The financial charges for initiation into the Order were as follows: under the age of 35 years, 2s. 6d.; 35 and under 38, 5s.; aged 38 and under 39, 6s. 6d.; 39 and under 40, 8s.; 40 and under 41, 11s.; 41 and under 42, 14s.; 42 and under 43, 17s.; 43 and under 44, £1; 44 and under 45, £1-5s.-0d.; 45, £1-10s.-0d.[5]

In addition to these charges, 'Tents' would regularly impose 'fines' on their members: after all, it was a strict organisation bound by moralistic guidelines!

A Rechabites jewel, celebrating their centenary in 1935.

5   Ibid., p. 219.

Regalia for the Order consisted of a sash worn over the right shoulder, and collars and sometimes aprons were also worn by certain officers. Some of the symbols used by the Order were the same as those used in Freemasonry, such as the Moon surrounded by seven stars; a Dove; the Sun; an intertwined Serpent; the All-seeing Eye; and Cross Keys, a Crown, a Lamb, a Tent, a sheaf of Corn and a Beehive.

The Order was originally intended for men only, but by 1836, within a year of its foundation, it was considered desirable to have a similar Order for women. Female tents were established in several parts of the country almost simultaneously, and medals were struck to commemorate the event. Having been instituted the cause spread, and when seven Tents had been formed a meeting of representatives was called and a governing body, to be known as the Executive Committee, was duly elected.

The first annual movable conference of the United Order of Female Rechabites was held in the British Schoolroom, Hanley, Staffordshire, on Saturday 11 August 1838, where delegates from female Tents in various parts of the country assembled and the progress of the Order during the past year was reported on. The prospect of the rapid spread throughout the country of the female IOR was much anticipated.[6] A code of general Rules, with a table of fines attached, was approved, ratified and confirmed, and the General Laws of the United Order of Female Rechabites were ordered to be printed. This code of rules fixed the titles of the female Tent officers as Senior Matron, Junior Matron, Past Senior Matron, Secretary, Treasurer, Stewardess, Levite and Guardian.[7]

The rituals seem to have varied from place to place but generally, as in Freemasonry, three Degrees were worked: Knight of Temperance, Knight of Fortitude, and Covenanted Knight of Justice. The ritual also had similar elements to Freemasonry, and the governing body, at least in England, was the Movable Committee, which met in different cities every two years. The first ''Making Book' or ritual of the Order was written by The Secretary of the first Tent, Bro. Joseph Thompson. It contained the opening and closing odes, Terminology (including some terms also used in Freemasonry), the 'making parts' for various officers, and a covenant for the candidate for admission to the Order.

It is interesting to note that under Rule 17 it says 'that *if any Brother of this Order thinks proper to enter any other Order, he shall have the privilege of doing so; and any*

---

6   Ibid., pp. 219-20.
7   Ibid., p. 220.

Tent shall be allowed to make a person belonging to any other secret Order, if in good health and character, and of a proper age, having signed to abstain from drinking all intoxicating liquors according to Rule 1. This enabled members of the IOR to join other Orders and, indeed, members of other Orders to join *them* – as long as they abstained from drink. Rule 18 goes on to say '*that no person under the age of nineteen years nor above forty-five shall be made a brother of this Order unless the son of a worthy brother who shall be allowed to be made at the age of eighteen*'.[8] Here there is a clear parallel with Freemasonry where the son of a Freemason, in good standing, may be made a Mason at the age of eighteen.

By 1839 the Order had spread to Scotland, with District No. 20 established in Edinburgh, and by 1841 the Order was present in Glasgow, Greenock, Aberdeen and Dundee, with a membership of 4,000 in 47 Tents.[9] By 1843 there were over 1000 tents and nearly 30,000 members, the society becoming commonplace in industrial towns in South Wales and in the north-west of England such as Salford, Manchester and Wigan. The Order was also present in Ireland and the Channel Isles. It also spread to the far corners of the British

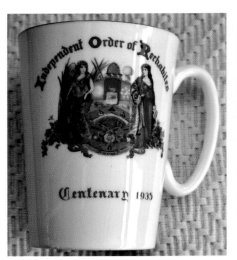 

The centenary Rechabite mug, front and reverse, revealing similar symbolism as used in Freemasonry, such as the All-seeing Eye and the Beehive.

8   Ibid., p. 24.
9   Ibid., p. 100.

RACOBITE WALKS BROAD O'TH LANE 1917

The Independent Order of Rechabites walking in procession through the village of Shevington, near Wigan in Lancashire, in 1917, wearing their sashes. Many thanks to the Shevington Conservative Club for supplying the photograph and to the Reprographics Department at Liverpool Hope University for the digital reproduction.

Empire, and by 1885 was present in Canada, Tasmania, Australia, New Zealand and Natal in South Africa. By 1893 the IOR could be found in Bengal in India and in Denmark. It later appeared on the Gold Coast, Nigeria, the Bahamas and in Germany. In the United States however the IOR fared poorly. There was also the Encamped Knights of Rechab of North America, which seems to have had a negligible impact, except locally in small areas.

With the repeal of prohibition in the United States the Rechabites collapsed, and in Britain the order diminished in size and influence after the development of the NHS. In 1999, the Society, by now known as the Rechabite Friendly Society, modernised and centralised its various local groups and regions into one Manchester- based Head Office. In 2004 the society opened up its membership to include temperate members or those who enjoy alcohol in moderation. Operating ever since under the name Healthy Investment, the society is now a modern financial service organisation committed to providing ethical savings and investment products.

Members of the IOR would take their pledge to be 'tee-total' extremely seriously, living life by their strict moral code. Indeed, Joseph Grime from Platt Bridge, Wigan, a staunch Rechabite, tells us in his memoirs that such was his feeling against the 'evils' of drink that he would avoid walking past the front of a public house and would also avoid walking over a trap-door leading into the cellar of a pub by crossing over the road, or even walking into the road itself to avoid the smell of alcohol.

Their influence was once so great that their membership in 1910 was recorded at 212,794 adults and 189,153 juvenile members. Overseas members were recorded at 44,380 adults and 19,361 juveniles. With the advent of the NHS after World War II the IOR began to suffer along with many other friendly societies, and Joseph Grime hinted at the difficulties faced by the members when he commented how he was suddenly paying twice for his cover – once in his fees for the society and then again in his National Insurance contributions. This may have echoed the feelings of many friendly society members, and one by one they gradually decided to lapse their membership.[10]

Daniel O'Connell, the Irish MP tries to Damage the IOR

In the history of this Order, one particular event stands out: an attack by Daniel O'Connell in 1844. O'Connell was a radical Irish Catholic politician, lawyer and one-time Freemason who defended the Craft against the Unlawful Oaths Bill under which all oath-based societies in Ireland were banned. O'Connell eventually left Freemasonry and formed the Catholic Association in 1823.

In 1840, he formed the Repeal Association to have the Act of Union between Great Britain and Ireland repealed. He eventually became a Member of Parliament for County Clare. As an MP he was expected to take a Protestant oath to be able to take his seat, but fought to have the Catholic Emancipation Bill passed and was thus able to take his seat in Parliament. He was highly regarded in Irish circles and held meetings at which it was not uncommon to have over 100,000 people attending. O'Connell was born in County Kerry in August 1775 and died in Genoa, Italy, *en route* to Rome, in May 1847.

His attack on the Rechabites took the form of a letter, which he sent to all the London newspapers, stating that the society was an '*unlawful, vicious, worthless institution*'. This of course was a shock to the Rechabite movement, and the Grand Secretary of the Order retaliated by sending a letter to all the newspapers which had published O'Connell's

10   *The Memoirs of Joseph Grime – a Rechabite from Platt Bridge, Wigan.* Private Collection.

attack. The Grand Secretary, William Grimshaw, was vociferous in his response to O'Connell, accusing him of having erroneous opinions and a judgement warped by prejudice, and arguing that he might have been misled in his attacks on the Order.

O'Connell had said in his letter that every individual member of the Rechabite Society was guilty of a transportable offence (meaning that if found guilty a person could be transported from Britain to one of its overseas colonies), something that was reminiscent of the Tolpuddle Martyrs. He concluded that the Rechabites were calculating and did great mischief among the working classes and that it was a vicious and worthless society. O'Connell also made a personal attack on an Irish Priest, Father Mathew, whom he stated did not approve of the society and kept himself clear of it.

Responding to the first charge of each member of the society being guilty of a transportable offence, the Grand Secretary challenged O'Connell's opinion as a lawyer, believing that it was founded in error. He compared the Rechabite movement, in law, to others such as the Oddfellows, Foresters, Druids, Shepherds, Gardeners and others, stipulating that any law or anything else which applied to any one of these orders must apply to all of them, and that they were not of an unlawful character as he had claimed. He went on to say that the Rechabites had dispensed with their secret signs and passwords and that they were much further removed from anything that might be considered more unlawful than the Oddfellows, who still retained their secret signs and passwords.

The Grand Secretary pointed out to O'Connell that letters from the society had previously been sent to both King George IV and William IV, and that these addresses had been acknowledged by their respective Ministers, Sidmouth and Peel. Had they been received from a society of an unlawful nature they would not have not been received in such a '*gracious manner*' by both their Majesties. He went further and drew O'Connell's attention to the fact that, in January 1837, Sir John Campbell, then Attorney-General, had been consulted on the lawfulness of the Order of Oddfellows and had concluded that '*I do not see any necessity for the Society being remodelled*'. The Grand Secretary pointed out that had he done so the members of the Rechabites also might have been guilty of a transportable offence, but they were not.

O'Connell's opinion was further alleged to have little weight because he did not seem to have noticed that if the Rechabite Society was unlawful then so was the Repeal Association, as the two were similar. Far from it being a worthless society, the Grand Secretary clearly indicated to O'Connell that each member was expected to exhibit perfect sobriety and good moral conduct. It taught them to be provident and to assist each other in times of distress, and that men of all creeds and political opinions are brethren and ought to dwell together in harmony.

With regard to Father Mathew, O'Connell had claimed that the Father did not approve of the Rechabites, but there is clear evidence to the contrary from a conversation with Grand Secretary Grimshaw, in which Father Mathew says *'that he had first become acquainted with the Rechabites in Glasgow, that he highly approved of the institution and he much regretted that the present state of Ireland precluded him from being instrumental in introducing so noble an institution into his own country'.* Grimshaw concluded by saying that, whilst O'Connell professed to be a friend of his country (Ireland) and its people, he was doing the work of the enemy by attempting to force submission. Finally he claimed that the Rechabites promoted concord and unity and were an unobjectionable benefit society identified with the Temperance cause. Nothing further was heard about the matter.[11]

Many other Temperance societies were founded, some of which were more localised, such as the Ashton-under-Lyne Temperance Society, which was founded in 1836. Other temperance societies were founded through local churches, such as the Methodists, Congregationalist and Baptists, although these churches and chapels seldom fully backed the societies. Along with being sternly opposed to alcohol, these churches were also against smoking, gambling and swearing, and were even sometimes known to oppose the popular Music Halls. One other society became synonymous with the temperance movement and became one of the leading moralistic organisations in the US – the Order of the Good Templars.

The Order of the Good Templars

The Good Templars was a society that advocated total abstinence from alcohol, and later became something of a political force and pressure group, campaigning for the restriction of the availability of alcohol and the curtailment of licensing hours for pubs. The Order was founded in America around 1851 following the formation of several temperance organisations such as the British Association for the Promotion of Temperance and the aforementioned Rechabites. In the 1840s, numerous temperance societies were founded in America and Britain, taking various forms, often following the pattern of Freemasonry by wearing regalia and conducting initiation ceremonies as well

---

11   Campbell, *History of the Rechabite Order*, p. 145.

FAR RIGHT: 'Love, Purity
and Fidelity', a jewel from
the Order of the Sons
of Temperance.

RIGHT: Cadets of
Temperance jewel
from June 1953.

as endowing further degrees. They were often termed
'Teetotallers Freemasonry'.

'The Sons of Temperance' was formed in America in
1841. It admitted women into its ranks, carried out degree
ceremonies, and had modes of recognition and passwords,
something that did not sit too well with some people in
the 'Teetotal' movement. The Order of the Templars was
formed originally as the 'Knights of Jericho' and later
changed its name to the Independent Order of Good
Templars. By 1868 there was a lodge of the Good Templars
in Birmingham, England, and by 1873 there was certainly a Grand Lodge of England
under the Independent Order of Good Templars.

Mark Tabbert, in his book *American Freemasons – Three Centuries of Building
Communities*, states that: '*The radical change taking place in the United States between the
election of President Andrew Jackson in 1828 and the end of the Civil War in 1865 brought
a blaze of new political, social, moral and religious organizations*'. These radical social
changes can also be seen in the United Kingdom: the social upheaval caused by the
Industrial Revolution created a need for men (and, indeed, women), to bond together
within new societies to share political and moral beliefs.

Many of the societies founded before 1840 had a moralistic aim: these included the
American Temperance Society, American Peace Society, General Union for Promoting
the Christian Observance of the Sabbath, American Lyceum Association, American
Anti-Slavery Society, American Home Mission Society and the American Sunday
School Union. Tabbert continues by quoting Arthur M. Schlesinger, *Biography of
a Nation of Joiners, The American Historical Review*, Vol. 50 No 10 (Oct 1944):

'Matters have come to such a pass, that a peaceable man can hardly venture to eat or drink, or go to bed or get up, to correct his children or kiss his wife, without obtaining the permission and direction of some…moral society'.

Some of these moralistic societies had an obvious Masonic influence: temperance organisations such as the 'Templars of Honor and Temperance' performed initiation rituals; wore regalia, aprons and sashes; and took oaths agreeing not to drink liquor or reveal the organisation's secrets. The most prominent of these societies was the 'Sons of Temperance', which grew to 6,000 lodges with 245,000 members within eight years of its founding in 1842. In the 1850s it temporarily surpassed Freemasonry as America's largest fraternal association.[12]

Many orders had 'Templar' in their title and, during this period, the Knights Templar legend was very popular, the chivalric image that the 'Templar' name conjured up being an obvious influence. The Good Templars had well-established lodges and, by 1858, a Right Worthy Grand Lodge of North America. Like Freemasonry, the Order had a system of three Degrees, which were never conferred unless at least seven degree members were present.

Their meetings also followed a similar pattern to Masonic lodge meetings, with an Order of Business. Usually this followed a regular pattern of:

1. Reading the Minutes
2. Reception of Communications or Petitions
3. Balloting on Applications
4. Initiation of Candidates
5. Reports of Committees
6. Miscellaneous Business

The opening of a lodge would be preceded by a prayer said by the lodge Chaplain.

Members could be admitted to the Order without going through a degree ceremony, but were obliged to have served at least six months' membership before being eligible to receive the degrees: by being connected with the Order for that length of time and having been bound to the principles of Total Abstinence they would be considered, by that stage, to be a fit and proper person to be admitted.

---

12   Tabbert, *American Freemasons*, pp. 73-74.

The degree ritual had similarities to that of Freemasonry and required a candidate to keep the ceremonies confidential, along with the secret signs, tokens and passwords. They also promised not to write, or cause to be written or indite, in part or in whole, any of the aforementioned private work of the degree ceremony.

There was a First Degree, followed by the Second Degree of Fidelity, with the third being the Degree of Charity. There was a further Degree, the Degree of Royal Virtue. At the close the senior officer present would announce to all present, whether man or woman:

> *'Brothers and Sisters...*
> *You will extend to this new associate your fellowship and regard. Unite with him in advancing the sacred cause of Temperance, in enlarging the spheres of human charity and love, and in a firm and implicit reliance upon Infinite Power and Infinite Mercy'.*

The Order was explicitly Christian in nature and, by 1858, each member of the Order taking the Degree of Charity was expected to take an obligation as follows:

> *'You........................, a member of the Order of Good Templars, in the presence of Almighty God, and these persons, do solemnly renew the Obligation of Total Abstinence, enjoyed in the initiatory work of this Order. You also promise to use all proper and lawful means in your power to promote the good of this Order, and advancement of the cause of Temperance. You further covenant to the extent of your ability, to inculcate the teachings of this Degree in your social intercourse, your example and in your daily life; and that you will keep from disclosure, upon improper occasions, and before those not entitled to know the same, any signs, passwords or private work of this Degree. You will in no case, write or cause to be written or indited, in part or in whole, any of the signs, passwords or tokens of this Degree, so that the same may be unlawfully obtained. You further promise in any and all relations you may sustain to this Temple, to seek the promotion of its best interest and the preservation of union, order and harmony in its deliberations. To all of which you pledge your sacred honor'.*

The Chaplain will invoke a Divine blessing upon the candidate:

Chaplain's Prayer

'O merciful Father, Creator and Preserver of the world, we implore Thee to grant us Thy presence and Thy countenance. Be pleased to bestow Thy benediction upon this person, who has taken upon himself the solemn obligation of this Degree and grant him grace and power to fill all its requirements and to regard all its injunctions...............etc.'.[13]

The Independent Order of the Good Templars also inspired the United Order of True Reformers, which was founded as the black version of the all-white Good Templars. This African-American Order was founded in Kentucky in 1872 and, like the black Orders that were founded in the likeness of the Elks and the Moose, it reveals how the black communities also had a need for fraternal societies and, in this case, an Order that

promoted total abstinence.[14] These black Orders were reminiscent of how Prince Hall Freemasonry had developed: like-minded African-American men (and sometimes women) came coming together in a similar cause or interest, and had modelled the Order on the existing one. In the case of Prince Hall Freemasonry, it was first recognised by the 'regular' Grand Lodge in London.

Today the Good Templars still survive as an international non-political society, working for the promotion of temperance, and are based in Sweden.

'Faith, Hope and Charity', a Good Templars breast ribbon from Lodge No. 3897, Ashton-under-Lyne.

---

13   Taken from C. W. Hamilton, *Degree Book – Order of Good Templars*, (The Right Worthy Grand Lodge of North America, 1858).

14   Beito, *From Mutual Aid to the Welfare State*, p. 36. For a comprehensive discussion of the Order see David M. Fahey, 'Why Some Black Lodges Prospered and Others Failed: The Good Templars and the True Reformers', in Matthew W. Hughey, (ed.), *Race and Ethnicity in Secret and Exclusive Social Orders: Blood and Shadow*, (London: Routledge, 2014), pp. 101-116.

THE ROYAL ANTEDILUVIAN ORDER OF BUFFALOES

One of the best known and largest of the fraternal societies is the Royal Antediluvian Order of Buffaloes. It is believed to have been formed in London by stage artists. Its motto, which has an obvious similarity to Masonry, is 'Unity, Liberty and Charity', the principles of the Order being Tolerance, Brotherly Love and Good Fellowship. It has similar regalia to Freemasonry and has its own degrees and ritual. The discussion of politics or religion at its meetings is forbidden which, again, is reminiscent of Freemasonry. The earliest known date of a Buffaloes lodge is the Harponian Lodge, founded in 1822, which met at the Harp Tavern, Great Russell Street, London, near the Drury Lane Theatre, London. As we shall see, some leading 'Buffs' were Freemasons and, of course, the present United Grand Lodge of England is situated in Great Queen Street, not far from Drury Lane.[1]

The exact origin of the Buffaloes is not entirely clear, and there is no mention of the Order prior to 1822, but they do appear to have a link to an older London- based club. In the late 18th Century there was a rather eccentric and boisterous club known as the City of Lushington, its membership consisting of actors and variety artists who held their meetings at various taverns in and around the many theatres of the day. The meeting-room would be laid out in the form of a 'City' with four 'Wards', while the Master was known as the 'Mayor' and his senior officers 'Aldermen'. Elections were held in the club, giving the 'City of Lushington' an air of independence, with Constables guarding the 'gates of the city', and canvassers bringing voters to the 'clerk of the poll'. The elections of the officers had a theatrical character and were reminiscent of other London clubs such as the Beef-Steak Club, which boasted 'Beef and Liberty' as its motto.[2]

1   M.W. Payne, *The Origin & Development of the Royal Antediluvian Order of Buffaloes*, (Leeds: John Blackburn Ltd., 1953), pp. 18-24.
2   See Harrison, *Genesis of Freemasonry*, p. 168. The Beef-Steak club was a semi-Masonic club that was described by James Boswell in his famous *Journal* and was frequented by MP John Wilkes.

The British actor and theatrical manager Sir Henry Irving was one such officer. Irving was also a Freemason and a member of Jerusalem Lodge No. 197 in London.

Membership of the Lushington Club was, however, denied to theatre technicians and stagehands, so they started to hold their own meetings. Pierce Egan, a well-known London theatre critic of the period, attributes the foundation of this new society to the artist Joseph Lisle and a comedian called William Sinnett.[3] Class distinctions therefore seem to have played a part in the origin of the Buffaloes, with the refusal to admit the Drury Lane staff leading to the foundation of a rival society, which, ironically, was to completely eclipse the Lushington Club. In his book *Finish to the adventures of Tom, Jerry and Logic*, published in 1828, Egan cites one of the aims of the new club as being the promotion of a '*hitherto neglected ballad*' called '*We'll chase the Buffalo*', a ballad that was still being sung in RAOB lodges as late as the 1950s.[4] There is evidence to show that several of the founders of the RAOB Grand Lodge of England were Freemasons, including Samuel Brown, who was a 'Primo' (Master) of the RAOB Beehive Lodge in Walworth circa 1865 and promoted the idea of a Grand Lodge; Samuel May of Temple Lodge No 101, London, a former Grand Steward of the United Grand Lodge England; and William Wade of St. Andrew's Lodge No 282, also of London.[5] The 'Buffalo Society' was thus derived from the Lushington Club and, as we shall see, certainly continued some of its traditions.

The names of the officers in the Buffaloes certainly echoed the legacy of the Lushington Club, as they had the prefix 'City' in the title, e.g. 'City Taster' or 'City Scavenger'. The City Taster had a most important role, as it was his responsibility to taste the ale in the establishment where they were meeting prior to proceedings commencing. If it was not up to the required standard the landlord would be '*fined two gallons of ale*' which was then consumed by the members present.[6] There is also reference to the '*partaking of weed*' at a convenient time early in the proceedings of the lodge session, though what this 'weed' actually was, and if it was somewhat different from the ordinary brand of tobacco, is not specified.[7] The society duly expanded as the

---

3   Payne, *Origin & Development of the Royal Antediluvian Order of Buffaloes*, pp. 21-3.
4   Ibid.
5   Ibid, pp. 61-3.
6   Ibid. See also Revd. Don Johnson, a paper submitted to the Masonic Province of East Lancashire, Short Paper Competition 2012. The Revd. is a Past Prov. Grand Sec for Lancashire RAOB.
7   Anon, *The Royal Antediluvian Order of Buffaloes Manual of Instruction*, (Leeds: Duffield Printers, 1983), pp. 10-11.

A selection of jewels from the Grand United Order of the Knights of the Golden Horn, which was in effect, a side-Order of the RAOB, formed in 1880. Their Encampments still meet. (Courtesy of Tapton Hall, Sheffield)

nineteenth century continued, mainly due to the granting of 'travelling dispensations' which allowed touring theatre-staff to set up lodges in various towns and cities throughout England and to initiate new members, one such famous lodge being the Shakespeare Lodge in Manchester.[8] With this growth came various splits and splinter societies: the Grand Lodge of England was formed in 1866, but two years later the Grand Surrey Banner Section broke away and then, in 1897, the Grand Lodge of England Limited Section also broke away from the original Grand Lodge of England. It is not known if the partaking of weed and excessive ale-tasting made any contribution to these splits.

The Order is similar to Freemasonry in that it has three administrative levels, namely Minor Lodges (Private), a Provincial Grand Lodge structure, and a Grand

---

8   Payne, *Origin & Development of the Royal Antediluvian Order of Buffaloes*, pp. 119-120.

Lodge, and four degrees of membership: the First Degree, known as a Kangaroo, the Second Degree or Certified Primo, the Third Degree or Knight Order of Merit, and the Fourth Degree or Roll of Honour. The Second Degree is awarded on the basis of a mixture of length of time in the Order, attendance and an examination in chairmanship skills, whilst the third and fourth degrees are based on length of membership and a proven attendance record. Provincial and Grand Lodge honours are not in the gift of the Chief Officer of the Province or Grand Lodge. To gain such an honour the member must have represented his Lodge as delegate to Provincial G.L. or represented his Province as a delegate to Grand Lodge, and must in addition to satisfactory length-of-service and attendance qualifications, have been elected to the Office by popular vote. The bizarrely named 'Kangaroo Degree' is so termed because the members jumped around the initiate, who was blindfolded with a bandage while seated on a chair. This comical scene was followed by a solemn march, with the Buffaloes carrying brooms, shovels, mops and a large kettle while reciting a chant that included the rather gruesome line '*Bloody-head and raw-bones…*'[9]

The Buffaloes, like Freemasonry and many of the other fraternal societies, which we have discussed, are philanthropic and charitable in nature, and lodges and provinces are at liberty to undertake whatever activity they consider appropriate to the needs of the community in which they work and live. The regalia of the RAOB is very similar to that of the Freemasons, consisting of aprons and a collar or sashes, and many members also wear breast-jewels. In addition, the Order also operates its own

A certificate from the RAOB, showing that the member was elected as a Knight of the Order of Merit.

rest- and convalescent-homes providing facilities for members, their wives and widows. Its headquarters are at Grove House in Harrogate, Yorkshire.

In a show of loyalty to the state, the Order decided to call itself the 'Loyal Order of the Buffaloes', and soon 'Loyal' became 'Royal', even though there has never been 'Royal' approval as such. The introduction of the Royal Warrant Act in the early 1900s required anyone using the 'Royal' prefix to register with the Lord Chancellor's Office and to stop using the title if permission to continue doing so was not granted. However, since the Buffaloes had been using the prefix from the 1840s the Lord Chancellor agreed that no objection would be raised on the continued use of the title on the grounds of long usage, provided no act by the Order arose which would disgrace its use.

In 1910, a committee was formed to look into the question of establishing convalescent-homes, and in 1924, the Order bought 'Elsinore' in Scarborough, on the north-east coast of Yorkshire. In the next decade two more followed, one near Weston-super-Mare and the other at Southport, Lancashire in 1945 (sold in 1972). So the Order of the Buffaloes had become more focused on its charitable and beneficent qualities, a far cry from the original eccentric drinking and smoking club! Two unrelated 'Buffalo' organisations were established in the United States: the Benevolent Order of Buffaloes was set up in New York in 1881 but became extinct by the early 1900s, while the Loyal Order of Buffalo was set up in Newark, New Jersey, in 1911. The latter was a fraternal benevolent association providing family physician services as well as death, sickness, accident and disability benefits – all for a $6 initiation fee and 75 cent monthly dues. Its Newark headquarters was called 'Home Range'. It too no longer exists.

The Buffaloes still exist in the UK however, and still have two convalescent-homes, which now have commercial aspects to them. Like Freemasonry and the other surviving fraternal societies in the UK, the 'Buffs' are in decline, with an estimated current active membership of 35-40,000. They do not accept women members, but women are active in a small affiliated group called the 'Lady Glades'. The headquarters of the Grand Lodge of the RAOB is currently based in Harrogate.[10]

The Buffaloes, at their conception in the 1820s, reflect the class differences inherent within the theatre. This professional snobbery helped ensure that they were strong

---

10 Correspondence between Andy Baker, Grand Tyler 2005, RAOB, GLE, and co-author Fred Lomax, dated 17 October 2014.

A selection of jewels from the RAOB, showing jewels presented for charity and attending convention as a delegate in the 1920s. *(Photo by David Harrison. Private collection)*

enough to survive amongst the fraternal organisations of the UK. From London they spread around England, with lodges being founded as far away as Liverpool and Manchester in the north. Like many of the other fraternal societies, such as the Oddfellows, Druids and Foresters, the Buffaloes suffered splits, but they still survive as a fraternal organisation to this day, albeit much reduced since their heyday in the nineteenth and early twentieth centuries.[11] They did however, influence a particular large Order in the USA, one that grew quickly and has become one of the most popular and enduring fraternal organisations in America: the Benevolent and Protective Order of the Elks.

---

11   The current website of the Order can be found at <www.raobgle.org.uk> [accessed 5 October 2014]

THE BENEVOLENT AND PROTECTIVE ORDER OF THE ELKS

This American Order was started by an English émigré who had once been a member of the Antediluvian Order of the Buffalo by the name of Charles Algernon Vivian. Vivian arrived in New York in 1867 and, having been a comic performer and singer in the music halls of London, he immediately set his sights on a similar career in the saloons of New York. He quickly met a number of other performers, actors and singers and they formed a club called the Jolly Corks, named after a trick using wine-bottle corks that Vivian had learnt in London.

Vivian was certainly a man of vision, and when a fellow-performer and friend died suddenly leaving a young wife and several children, the Jolly Corks decided to form a benevolent society. Vivian wanted to call this new Order the Buffaloes in an obvious nod to his membership of the Order back in England. However, another American animal was suggested, and a vote was taken to decide between Buffalo and Elk, with Elk winning the day. Thus, the Benevolent and Protective Order of the Elks was born, quickly growing throughout the USA, and after twenty years had 100 lodges with over 10,000 members. Vivian left New York for the Western states, where he died of pneumonia in Leadville, Colorado in 1880, aged just 34. He is still held in high regard by the Elks today as the initial founder of the Order.[1]

Vivian's story as recited in his biography written by his widow and published after his death reflected that of many of the immigrants who came to the USA seeking a new life in a new world after being lured by the American Dream.[2] Vivian soon sought out like-minded men to form a club, and it was within the security of this club that they could bond together and help each other during a time of uncertainty and hardship. This was, indeed, a story that not only mirrored the societies that were

---

1   J. Herbert Klein, *All About the Order of Elks*, (Los Angeles: International FA Publishing, 2011), pp. 15-44.
2   See Imogen Holbrook Vivian, *A Biographical Sketch of Charles A. S. Vivian*, (1904).

formed in the USA but those in the UK also: societies such as the Buffaloes and the IOR were founded by men who not only wanted to socialise with like-minded gentlemen but sought to meet their needs, be it the promotion of temperance, protection in sickness or benevolence. To quote an old Trade Union motto, 'United we stand'. The Elks went from strength to strength and, like Freemasonry, had a ritual, used signs and symbols, and became a society where men could join and contribute to their growing community, something that was reflected in the various fraternal societies of the UK, which contributed to the developing communities of the industrial towns in which they were based.

The society also inspired other Orders, especially across the racial divide. In 1898, Alpha Lodge No. 1 of the Improved Benevolent and Protective Order of the Elks of the World in Cincinnati, Ohio, was founded by two black men named Arthur J. Riggs and Benjamin Franklin Howard. The idea was to organise a society for up-and-coming black men that would have a focus for education and patriotism and which would help the community, not unlike the concept of Prince Hall Masonry in the USA a century before. Riggs and Howard used the 'original' Elks as their model, and adapted its ritual, which, surprisingly, was not copyrighted. However, the 'original' Elks took a dislike to the move: almost a decade of legal wrangling followed, and Riggs had to leave Cincinnati after receiving threats. The 'black' Elks, however, kept the name, and created a charter for the new organisation, which, between 1898 and 1906, grew to include 100 lodges in twenty states. The Order also extended its interests in early civil rights: they founded a Civil Liberties department in 1926 that opposed segregation and promoted integration.[3]

The overall appeal of the Elks and its ethos of brotherly love, relief and charity helped establish it as one of the most influential and, indeed, one of the largest fraternal organisations in the USA. Today the organisation is still at the centre of the community: the Order has 'community centres' up and down the country, which provide essential amenities such as a bar, committee-rooms and meeting-rooms, while charity and relief are still central concerns of the society. The Order is now open to

3   See Tamara L. Brown, Gregory S. Parks and Clarenda M. Phillips, (ed.), *African American Fraternities and Sororities: The Legacy and the Vision*, (Kentucky: The University Press of Kentucky, 2012). See also Theda Skocpol, Ariane Liazos and Marshall Ganz, *What a Mighty Power We Can Be: African American Fraternal Groups and the Struggle for Racial Equality*, (Princeton: Princeton University Press, 2006), pp. 179-181, and Nina Mjagkij, (ed.), *Organizing Black America: An Encyclopedia of African American Associations*, (London: Routledge, 2003), p. 231.

women members, which has boosted the membership and made the lodges more family-friendly[4] and, despite the tensions between the 'black' Elks and the original Order back in the late nineteenth century, the society now welcomes African-Americans. The society has attracted Presidents such Harry S. Truman and John F. Kennedy, and Hollywood actors such as Clint Eastwood.[5]

4   Klein, *About the Order of Elks*, pp. 179-180.
5   Ibid., pp. 72-88.

THE LOYAL ORDER OF THE MOOSE

This popular American fraternal society, like the Elks, was named after another strong and robust American mammal to symbolise the USA, strength and unity. The moose is a mammal that only takes what it needs to survive and is protective by nature, which symbolised what the new society was all about. The Order was started in 1888 in Louisville, Kentucky, by a certain Dr John Henry Wilson, a local physician. A number of lodges were founded, including ones in St. Louis and Cincinnati, but by the beginning of the 1900s, Dr Wilson had become disillusioned with the Order and had left.

The Moose went into rapid decline, and by 1906 there were only two lodges left in Indiana. The society was saved by a Welsh émigré called James J. Davis, a hard-working man who had been an 'iron puddler' in the steel mills of Pennsylvania since childhood. He joined the Moose as its 247th member, and quickly saw the potential in the Order: the society would become a 'self-help' organisation, providing cover for sickness, funeral payments for the widow and children of deceased members, and benefits for widows if their husbands became disabled. Davis, who somewhat overshadowed the work of Wilson, also started the 'Mooseheart' – a centre for the education of children of deceased members.

By 1912, the Order had grown from 247 members and two lodges in one State to 500,000 members and more than 1000 lodges throughout the USA. By 1913, women could also join, with the 'Women of the Moose' being founded. This led to a more family-oriented society, and the society continued to move forward, creating 'Moosehaven' – a centre for retired Moose members. The Order grew accordingly and, in 1926, the Loyal Order of the Moose was established in the UK, a Grand Lodge being founded at the birthplace of Davis in Tredegar in Wales.[1]

---

1   Correspondence between Roger M.L. Williams, current Secretary to the Management Committee of Moose International British Headquarters, and co-author Fred Lomax, dated 1 October 2014. Moose International still survives in the UK, its headquarters being based in Winscombe, Somerset. See the official website: <www.mooseintl.org.uk> [accessed 6 October 2014]

An extract from Moose magazine referring to Women of the Moose.
(Photograph by David Harrison)

The success of the Moose was down to the recognition that, as in the UK before the advent of the welfare state, there was a need for security and protection for working-class families. Membership of the Moose also provided a family-friendly and Christian community to be a part of, supplied a social focus, and was an organisation that included both men and women. Davis turned his attention to politics and, in 1930,

A Moose's head on the wall at the Moose bar in Salem, Massachusetts.

(Photograph by David Harrison)

was elected to the US Senate where he fought on behalf of the Unions, becoming a leading light in the passing of ground-breaking legislation that forced building contractors to pay labourers prevailing Union-level wages in any government construction work.

Now known as Moose International, the Moose is still going strong in the US and Canada, and still has still a presence in the UK. Like the Elks, they have 'community centres' in various towns and cities with a bar, meeting-rooms – usually with a Moose's head on the wall – and a function-room. Various sports activities are also linked to the organisation. The Order has a ritual, secret passwords, and ceremonies, such as the 9 o'clock ceremony, when all members turn towards 'Mooseheart' and say the prayer 'Suffer little children' at the same time as the children of 'Mooseheart' also kneel in prayer. Similarities with the Masonic 9 o'clock Toast and the Elks' 11 o'clock Toast (taken later due to the fact that the Elks were formed by stage performers who worked late) are evident, though the Masonic and Elks' toast is in homage to absent brethren.[2] The Moose, like the Masons, also ask their candidates if they believe in a Supreme Being, and then take an obligation.

Like the Elks before them, in 1925 the Loyal Order of the Moose came into legal conflict with an African-American Order inspired by the Moose calling themselves the Independent, Benevolent and Protective Order of the Moose. This 'black' Moose was an attempt to form a fraternal society modelled on the 'original' Moose and, again, reflected the need for similar societies in the black communities of America. A ruling that they had to cease using the name 'Moose' ensued, but they were allowed to use the same Office titles and colours as the original Order.

Despite suffering greatly during the Great Depression, the Moose did not abolish sick and funeral benefits, and with the increase in unemployment and decrease in membership, it became a difficult time, not only for the Moose but also for other fraternal societies. The Moose showed commitment to their valued members when they helped them to pay off arrears and, in doing so, they weathered the storm. Today they remain one of the largest fraternal organisations in the US.[3] The charitable and philanthropic ethos of the Moose certainly inspired and captivated the interest of working men and women and, like the Elks, its membership has included Presidents such as Franklin D. Roosevelt and Harry S. Trueman, and actors such as Charlie Chaplin and Ernest Borgnine.

2   See Klein, *About the Order of Elks*, p. 113-5.
3   Beito, *From Mutual Aid to the Welfare State*, pp. 231-2.

THE DRUIDS

The very name of the Druids conjures up visions of mystical rituals in stone circles, and indeed it was this particular romantic vision of the ancient Druids that fuelled imaginations during the eighteenth century, leading writers such as Thomas Paine and William Stukeley to comment on the links between Druidism and Freemasonry, both writers recognising similarities between the supposed sun worship of the Ancient Druids and the ritual of Masonry.[1] By the late 18th and early 19th centuries many legends had been formed concerning the origins of Freemasonry, with links to the Druids being discussed by Paine and the Welsh Bard Iolo Morganwg,[2] and these views in turn influencing other writers on Freemasonry, such as Richard Carlile, who added their own interpretations to the 'history', with Carlile reflecting that Freemasonry was connected with *the ancient Pagan mysteries*.[3] During the 19th century the three main Druid friendly societies – the Ancient Order of Druids, the United Ancient Order of Druids and the Order of Druids – became as popular as the Oddfellows and the Foresters, with members finding both financial security and a ritualistic pathway to enlightenment.

Interest in the ancient Druids flourished during the eighteenth century. The Cymmrodorion Society, for example, founded in 1751, celebrated Welsh culture and literature, with the Freemason Watkin Williams Wynn, the fourth Baronet, as Chief President, dressing ceremoniously in Druid's robes when attending London masquerades.[4] The Williams Wynn family had been ardent Jacobite supporters in

---

1   See Thomas Paine, *Origin of Free Masonry*, in *The Works of Thomas Paine*, (New York: E. Haskell, 1854) and William Stukeley, *Stonehenge a temple restor'd to the British Druids*, (W. Innys and R. Manby, 1740).

2   Iolo Morganwg (1747-1826), a Glamorgan stonemason, revived his own version of the Welsh Druidic Order, creating a ritual which, though based on sun worship and stone circles, had a content which hinted at a Masonic influence. Morganwg became a popular Welsh radical, and a midsummer meeting of his Druid *Gorsedd* was held in Primrose Hill, London, in 1792. He also supported Thomas Paine, composing a song on the Rights of Man. See Elijah Waring, *Recollections and Anecdotes of Edward Williams, the Bard of Glamorgan; or Iolo Morganwg*, (London: Charles Gilpin, 1850). Also see Philip Jenkins, *A History of Modern Wales*, (London: Longmans, 1992), pp. 181-4.

3   Carlile, *Manual of Freemasonry*, p. xiv.

4   Harrison, *Genesis of Freemasonry*, p. 174.

A 'medallion' revealing a hooded Druid, issued by the Provincial Grand Lodge of Ancient Druids, Yorkshire, 1815. The style is similar to the famous 'Anglesey Druid' coin which had been minted for the workers of the Parys Mine in the 1790s.

Wales, and had been involved in the secret Jacobite club 'The Circle of the White Rose'. In 1822, the Cymmrodorion Society began to publish its Transactions and, along with its North Welsh counterpart The Gwyneddigion, founded in 1770, it attracted the attention of radical Welshmen, such as the Paineite John Jones, also known as 'Jac Glan-y-Gors'.[5]

The resurgence of interest in the Druids can also be seen in the activities of the Welsh poet and scholar Iolo Morganwg, who founded the *Gorsedd* in the later eighteenth century. In 1792 Morganwg, who claimed links to the ancient Druids, performed a mysterious ceremony on Primrose Hill in London. He was subsequently linked to Freemasonry by later writers, and he was certainly inspired by the radical writings of Thomas Paine. This early event on Primrose Hill is now seen as the beginning of the modern National Eisteddfod.[6] Freemasonry certainly seemed to have inspired elements of the regalia, symbolism and ritual of the new Druids, e.g. the Eisteddfod held at Mold in 1873, while in Liverpool in 1884 the *Gorseddogion* wore ceremonial dress such as aprons and sashes, which is instantly reminiscent of Masonic and Friendly Society regalia.

---

5   Jenkins, *History of Modern Wales*, p. 181-4.
6   Ibid., p. 182.

The Ancient Order of Druids, the United Ancient Order of Druids, and the Order of Druids

The Ancient Order of Druids was formed as a Friendly Society at the King's Arms in London in 1781, and soon began to spread its influence, forming new 'lodges'. Even though the Society suffered in the wake of the Secret Societies Act of 1799, it began to grow again in the early nineteenth century and, by 1831, had 200,000 members. However, as the lodges spread throughout the country, new ideas were put forward, and democratic reforms were suggested. The Ancient Order of Druids thus split into two, leading to the foundation of the United Ancient Order of Druids in 1833.[7] In 1858, another split occurred when the Order of Druids was founded from lodges that broke away from the original body of the Ancient Order of Druids. The Order of Druids was based in the industrial 'Districts' of Cheshire, Lancashire and Yorkshire, such as Crewe, Manchester, and Sheffield (which was the largest 'District'). The Druids' Sheffield Friendly Society still exists today, and is the result of the various Districts amalgamating and consolidating in recent years due to the declining membership of the lodges, though it is now purely a mutual financial organisation.[8] The United Ancient Order of Druids became extremely successful at expanding overseas, especially in Australia and the USA, and along with the Ancient Order of Druids still has some lodges operating in England.

The ritual and symbolism used in the Druid lodges was somewhat similar to Freemasonry. An example of the similarity in the symbolism used in Freemasonry and

The sign of the Druid Inn, Gorsedd in North-east Wales. This is one of three pubs named the Druid Inn in close proximity to each other, all dating from the later nineteenth century. The sign shows the typically romantic scene of robed Druids performing a ceremony in a stone circle. Just over the road from the pub is a standing stone called the Druid Stone. There is also a 'Druid Inn' at Birchover in Derbyshire, which is located near to the 'Rowter Rocks', where, according to local tradition, the ancient Druids practised rituals.

(*Photograph by David Harrison*)

---

7   See Andrew Prescott, 'THE VOICE CONVENTIONAL: Druidic Myths and Freemasonry', a paper given to the Kirkcaldy Masonic Research Conference, May 2001, and at the Fourth International Conference of the Canonbury Masonic Research Centre, November 2002, <http://www.lodgehope337.oorg.uk/lectures/prescott%20S01.PDF> [accessed 20 August 2009]. See also Owain Morgan, *Pabell Dofydd Eglurhad ar anianyddiaeth grefyddol yr hen dderwyddon Cymreig*, (Caerdydd: argraffwyd gan Daniel owen d'I ywmni, 1889), in which Morgan describes the history of the Druid Order in Wales.

8   See <http://www.druidsfriendly.com/about.htm> [accessed 16 July 2012]

LEFT AND RIGHT:
Selection of jewels from the
Ancient Order of Druids

the Druid Orders can be seen in the Druid symbol for Awen /I\ – a Welsh word for inspiration (poetic or musical) which describes the inspiration of the bards in Welsh poetic tradition, and which is reminiscent of the radiating downward light, which emits from the All-Seeing-eye in Freemasonry. Other Druid symbols that have a similarity to Masonic symbolism include the use of the skull and the tree of life. A belief in a supreme being is also a necessity for joining the Order. It was also forbidden to discuss religion and politics within the lodge room, just as in Freemasonry.[9]

The Druids could also interrelate with other friendly societies, such as when representatives visited the Victoria Lodge of Oddfellows at Leigh during a presentation for Mr. H. Brooks – one of the oldest members of the lodge – held at a 'club room' in the Queen's Arms. The Victoria Lodge of Oddfellows was at the time a thriving lodge, and a relationship was evident, not only with the local Druids, but also with the Foresters, as a report of the event noted when quoting a rather spirited speech on the ethos of all the friendly societies and their ultimate purpose:

---

9   Morgan, *Pabell Dofydd Eglurhad ar anianyddiaeth grefyddol yr hen dderwyddon Cymreig*, (Caerdydd: argraffwyd gan Daniel owen d'I ywmni, 1889). Morgan uses the Awen symbol on the cover of his work along with the symbol of the skull set within a megalithic burial chamber.

*'If a man paid into the Oddfellows, Druids, Foresters, or any other kindred
society, he not only laid up for himself the honestly earned reward of his
prudence and forethought, but he entitled himself to a right in case of need'.*[10]

Like Freemasonry, the revived interest in the Druids filtered into the minds of the
nineteenth century Welsh people, and many public houses began to be named after
them. An example of this popular romantic interest in the Druids can be seen with
three existing Druid Inns in North-east Wales: one in the atmospheric setting of
Llanferris; one just a few miles away in the village of Pontblyddyn; and another
situated in the aptly-named village of Gorsedd near Holywell. All three date from the
Victorian period. Even in England, at Birchover in Derbyshire, a Druid Inn can be
found set within a mysterious landscape of legend and tradition. A lodge of the
Ancient Order of Druids met there for some time in the nineteenth century.

The Druids and the Eisteddfod

The Druidical career of Dr William Price is an example of a Welsh radical who embraced the romantic ideology of the ancient Druids to put forward his idea of a Welsh identity. Price, like Iolo Morganwg before him, forged a romantic view of the past: for example, he traced the roots of Greek civilisation to the Pontypridd area, where he was also a Chartist leader and became a supporter of local miners' organisations and co-operative movements. His desire for ritual and what he perceived to be the ancient practices of the Druids, came to a climax when he cremated his deceased son 'Jesus Christ' Price in 1884; in doing so Price became a pioneer for cremation in Britain. As a self-appointed Archdruid, Price was seen regularly, such as when he visited the Llangollen Eisteddfod in 1858 wearing his self-styled ceremonial regalia, which included a fox-fur headdress and the obligatory Druid robes. His eccentricity and fame came with a healthy appetite for women, which resulted in a number of children, some even fathered late in life. He was also involved in the Chartist Newport rising of 1839, Price's political radicalism going hand-in-hand with his radical views on Druidical ideology and his ideas on Welsh national identity.

The National Eisteddfod was an event that certainly captured the romantic nature of Welsh culture, the *Gorsedd* being an integral part of the festival. Today there are three Orders in the *Gorsedd* – the Order of Ovates, the Order of Bards, and the Order of Druids – and there is still an emphasis on Welsh poetry in the Bardic tradition. The early Eisteddfods took place in various locations throughout Wales, such as Llangollen in 1858 and Llandudno in 1896, as well as Liverpool in 1884, the Liverpool gathering being largely due to the sizeable Welsh population of the port, though various smaller unofficial 'Eisteddfod' events took place in Wales. One such local example was held on Bardsey Island off the Llyn Peninsula in 1873, and was, by all accounts, a lively event with lots of drink and with brass bands from Pwllheli and Caernarfon providing the music.

Bardsey also had its own 'king' during the nineteenth and early twentieth centuries, the king being crowned with a tin crown during a ceremony reminiscent of a more ancient time. The king was expected to fulfil a position of leadership amongst the people of the island. Bardsey Island is steeped in tradition: it is supposed to be the burial-place of the legendary King Arthur, and was a place of pilgrimage during the medieval period. The king of Bardsey certainly had a place of honour during the Eisteddfod on the island, though the king that oversaw the event – John Williams II – was deposed in 1900 for being a drunkard.

An Eisteddfod chair dating from 1915.

(Photograph by David Harrison)

Another Eisteddfod chair, from 1923.

(Photograph by David Harrison)

RIGHT: An AOD past services jewel revealing the 'shaking of hands' symbol. This symbol is found on many gravestones from the nineteenth and twentieth centuries.

BELOW: Another AOD jewel revealing the symbolism of the acorn – a popular symbol in Druidism representing fertility, life and rebirth.

THE ROYAL ANCIENT ORDER OF FORESTERS, THE ANCIENT ORDER OF FORESTERS AND THE INDEPENDENT ORDER OF FORESTERS

Like the Druids, Buffaloes and the Oddfellows, the original Royal Ancient Order of Foresters broke up into a number of independent Orders, with the Ancient Order of Foresters being situated in England and the Independent Order of Foresters in America and Canada. Both of these breakaway Orders attracted working men, had the same fraternal and beneficial benefits as the Oddfellows and Druids, and expanded rapidly in the changing industrial climate of the late nineteenth century.

The RAOF is believed to have originated in Yorkshire, and there is evidence to show that a 'Court' (lodge) existed in Leeds as early as 1790. Other Courts were formed, and the Order then adopted the more loyal title of the Royal Ancient Order of Foresters. By 1834, following several years of discontent, a breakaway group was formed in Rochdale called the Ancient Order of Foresters. Like many other Friendly and Fraternal societies in that period it had two sides to the organisation: the friendly society which supplied the insurance side, and the fraternal side which, to a point, followed the model of Freemasonry. The Ancient Order of Foresters adapted and based its ritual on Biblical events, although the officers of a Court used rather romantic titles such as Chief Ranger, Senior Woodward, Junior Woodward, and Beadle. Courts were guarded by two Beadles and by the Senior and Junior Woodward, whose job was to serve all summonses, visit the sick, dispense allowances and take charge of all court property. The regalia of the Beadles included huge cow-horns slung from the left shoulder and axes, while each Woodward also carried an axe.[1]

---

1   The Leigh Journal, November 1886, Leigh Local Studies, WLCT.

Procession of the Ancient Order of Foresters, dressed romantically as ancient woodsmen, with feathers in their hats and on horseback.

The regalia of the Order consisted of sashes, collars, collarettes and jewels in a wide variety of styles. The regalia have changed over the years, but generally, they have been 'forest' green. It is however true to say that, at certain times in its history, the Order in Britain has seen its members dressed in elaborate uniform comprising wide-brimmed hats, slightly reminiscent of those worn by the Musketeers of France, along with long coats with broad leather belts, gauntlets and long leather boots. This style of dress can still be seen in a photograph from 1928, though in a later photograph from 1938 the members are dressed in ordinary suits.

By the 1860s, the AOF's financial state was healthy enough for it to be able to engage in general charity work as well as providing financial support for its members. Foresters regularly raised money for lifeboat services and the provision of life-saving apparatus on sea coasts, and in 1862 they voted to raise £500 to help depressed textile manufacturing regions. The Leigh Chronicle reported in July 1873, that '*The object is one well worthy of the support of the public and a very praiseworthy step on behalf of the society in thus providing additional and sufficient support for the aged infirm and distressed members in trying times of need instead of permitting them to become pauperised and a burden to the ratepayers at large'.[2]*

As the working population of England expanded during the nineteenth century so the need for security grew and, like the Druids and Oddfellows, the Ancient Order of Foresters grew with it. The Order became a very successful organisation, and the Executive Council reported on 1 December 1872 that it comprised 254 Districts and 4,080 subordinate Courts with 421,988 financial members and 8,770 honorary members. The amount of Grand Court funds totalled £1,849,513, the equivalent of £170,000,000 in 2012. The average membership of the Courts was reported at 103.[3] An excerpt from the Leigh Chronicle of 19 April 1873 shows the extent to which the Ancient Order of Foresters had grown:

'THE ANCIENT ORDER OF FORESTERS
A meeting at Tyldesley, Lancashire – Statistics of the Order

The importance of friendly societies as a means of affording assistance in times of sickness and difficulty is now fully recognised that it is no longer necessary to defend them from those mistaken notions, which formerly prevailed respecting them.

By steady perseverance difficulties have steadily been overcome and the Great Orders have now their courts and lodges in every town and village in the country. On the Continent too and in the colonies, the great principle of mutual assistance has been worked out successfully, so that a Forester or an Oddfellow can scarcely find a place where he will not discover a court or lodge ready and willing to render him help. There are still many working men who are not members of any society, but their number is gradually decreasing, as is evident by the fact that the increase to the Ancient Order of Foresters for the twelve months ending December 1st 1872 amounted to no less than 25,744 financial and 613 honorary members.

---

2   The Leigh Chronicle, July, 1873, Leigh Local Studies, WLCT.
3   The Leigh Journal, 1 December 1872, Leigh Local Studies, WLCT.

The usual quarterly meeting of the 'Leigh District' of the above Order composed of delegates from courts 'St. George's Tyldesley, 'Leigh Glory' and 'Leigh Unity', 'St Peter's Glory', Culcheth, 'Massey's Glory' Lately Common and 'Pride of Atherton' Atherton; and the district officers for the time being, was held at the Seven Stars Inn, Castle Street, Tyldesley, on Saturday evening last week.

The usual preliminaries having been gone through, the auditors proceeded to examine the accounts and after carefully going through the same certified to the financial condition of the District being in every way satisfactory and to the Courts being generally in a very prosperous state......'[4]

Obviously, from the above report it can be seen that the friendly and fraternal societies were providing a very valuable service by way of sickness and injury benefit and a funeral fund for their members. The following statistics from the Leigh Journal of 26 November 1886, albeit some 14 years later, help confirm this:

'Lancashire Forestry – the Ancient Order of Foresters, according to the official statistics just compiled by Mr. Secretary Shawcross, on the 1st of January 1886, had in Lancashire a total of 276 courts, with 22,936 members, having a capital of £91,385, and an annual revenue of £20,224 from members' contributions and £2,984 from interest on capital. The previous year's payments for benefits amounted to £20, 648 – £14,174 for sick benefits and £6,474 for funeral benefits.

The Manchester district, the strongest in the country, consisted of 70 courts, with 5,689 members and a capital of £15,377. Last year the revenue was £7,411 – £5,388 from members' contributions and £2,023 from interest on capital. The payment of benefits last year amounted to £5,376 – £3,240 for sick and £2,138 for funeral benefits. There are several other good districts in the country, but there are some 60 courts not committed to any district, isolation that the Order now discourages, because the area is too small to equalise funeral liabilities'.[5]

4   The Leigh Chronicle, 19 April 1873, Leigh Local Studies, WLCT.
5   The Leigh Journal, 26 November 1886, Leigh Local Studies, WLCT.

These societies not only provided financial security to its members but also provided social activities from which not just the members but the general public benefited as well: there was an example of this in August 1873 when the Ancient Order of Foresters organised a Grand Gala and Picnic in Leigh, Lancashire. The Leigh Chronicle of 9 August 1873 reported:

'*FORESTERS GALA AND PICNIC*
The Leigh District of the Ancient Order of Foresters' Friendly Society held a grand gala and picnic in Atherton Park, on Saturday last, the main object of which was the formation of a Benevolent Fund for the aged, distressed, and infirm members of the Order.

Two birds were thus killed with one stone – while an object worthy of all praise, and deserving the support of every one, was being carried out, the general public had at the same time afforded them an opportunity to participate in an afternoon's innocent recreation and amusement.

The district consists of six courts, and at the present time, we are informed, numbers some 400 members. The Tyldesley and Atherton Courts arrived in Leigh by way of Kirkhall Lane, headed by the Tyldesley Catholic Band; whilst those of Culcheth and Lately Common arrived by way of Bedford, headed by St. Joseph's Catholic Band.

Arriving in Leigh, the members dispersed for the purpose of obtaining refreshments, after which they re-assembled in the Market Place, and headed by their bands, and carrying flags, banners, banner[e]ts, and other insignia of the Order, formed a procession through Market Street, King Street to Pennington Church, returning thence down Bradshawgate, through Union Street, Lord Street, and by way of Bedford Leigh Station into Bedford, as far as Butts Bridge, back through Bradshawgate, Market Street, through to the Avenue, and thence to the park.

About 30 members were on horseback, dressed in full regalia. In the procession were the representatives of the celebrated Ranger of Sherwood Forest, the bold Robin Hood, Little John, his right hand man, Friar Tuck, Cain and Abel, Shepherd and his dogs, and a number of other officials whose name and position in the Order – not having ourselves being initiated into the mysteries of Forestry – we did not understand.

The procession through the streets, as processions of a novel character always do, attracted the attention of admiring thousands, and probably caused more than one looker-on to resolve to at once apply to have his name enrolled on the list of the members of the Society. The day was beautifully fine. Had those who fixed the arrangements written to the clerk of the weather in reference to the proceedings, they could not have resolved to hold the gala on a more favourable occasion, so far as atmospheric influences were concerned.

Arrived in the park, the sports commenced. These consisted of foot and sack racing, high leaping, and other exercises for well-trained athletes; but a salute to the all-but-omnipresent 'Aunt Sally' who delights to poke her nose into all gatherings where a bit of fun is going on, dancing and archery, were by far the most popular amusements. We have not heard what the day's proceedings are likely to raise for the fund, but we trust it will be something handsome.

There was a good gathering of persons on the ground taking part in the various recreations that had been provided for them, and everything passed off in the most satisfactory manner. Opportunities for innocent and health-giving amusements do not occur too frequently among us, and we hope the present is not the last time the Foresters will hold their gala in Atherton Park or in the neighbourhood. Several gentlemen have, we understand, signified their intention of becoming honorary members of the Order'.[6]

Social occasions did not always involve members of the public, and the Order of Foresters, like many other fraternal orders, held anniversary dinners in local pubs. A court would organise a dinner for the members to which ladies were sometimes invited. Court affairs would be discussed, especially their financial state, along with any local initiatives which were taking place, after which there was entertainment with the usual drinking, music and dancing. Here is a report of a dinner held at the Bucks Head, Abram, Lancashire, in August 1884:

'ANCIENT ORDER OF FORESTERS (No. 1549)
On Monday last, the members of this court held their anniversary and forming a procession started from the Buck's Head, Abram, about half-past

---

6   The Leigh Chronicle of 9 August 1873, Leigh Local Studies, WLCT.

nine. They proceeded through Bickershaw Lane, Hindley Green, Hindley, Low Green and Lower Ince back to head-quarters.

The procession consisted of about 100 members, of which about sixty were on horseback and looked immense, the older members in wagonettes. On their return they sat down to a substantial dinner catered for by Mrs. Pimblett, which was in every respect a success.

After the removal of the cloth, Bro. William Magnall was voted to the chair, supported by Bro. John Higson, Junr. After the usual Loyal Toasts, the Health of the Hostess was proposed and received heartily for the splendid spread she had set before them.

The remainder of the evening was spent in singing and dancing, &c. and the part broke up a little before eleven highly satisfied with the work the committee had done that day.[7]

Quality housing was also an issue for the working families in the ever-developing industrial centres, and the Foresters that met at the Buck's Head were again leading the way with providing social support in the area by contributing to the development of a row of cottages. There is still a row of eight 'Foresters' cottages along Warrington Road, Abram, Wigan, which were built in 1893, and which have a plaque on the wall of one of the cottages which states:

'*Erected by Court Faithful Abraham No. 1549 of the Ancient Order of Foresters As a Memento of their Jubilee 1893*'.

They are situated at 437 Warrington Road onwards and are within a short walking distance from the Bucks Head, where the Foresters used to meet. In fact, an article in the Leigh Journal of 23 June 1893 reported that a Jubilee procession had taken place on a fine summer's day and that the Foresters had, after passing through many local communities, returned to the Buck's Head, dismounted from their horses after a distance of nearly fifteen miles, and made their way to the site of the cottages to witness

---

7   Miscellaneous newspaper report of the dinner held at the Bucks Head, Abram, Lancashire, in August 1884. Leigh Local Studies, WLCT.

The Foresters Cottages, Abram near Wigan, dated 1893.

the stone-laying ceremony. The article also mentions that the Foresters had previously invested some of their surplus income into erecting cottages in nearby Platt Bridge, but sadly, these have not been located.[8]

It appears that the social aspect of being a Forester was a vitally important feature of the Order, though sometimes not everything went quite as well as it should, and there is a record of a court case being brought against a member of the Foresters for allegedly obtaining benefits to which he was not entitled.

The Leigh Chronicle of 29 January 1876 reported the following:

8   The Leigh Journal, 23 June 1893, Leigh Local Studies, WLCT.

'ALLEGATIONS AGAINST A FORESTER

At the Town Hall, Leigh on Monday before Jabez Johnson, Esq. and a bench of magistrates, William Walmesley, Bolton, was summoned by John Smith, Tyldesley, for fraudulently obtaining £2, belonging to Court 'St. George' No. 283 of the Ancient Order of Foresters (Leigh District).

Mr. Ambler appeared for the prosecution and the said complainant is a representative of the Court of St. George of the Ancient Order of Foresters in Tyldesley. On the 13th January, in this present year, the defendant saw the complainant, who was an officer of the society, in relation to receiving some funeral money, payable at the death of his mother. According to the rules of the Leigh District, under which the Court is governed, it is provided that at the death of member's widow, the relatives shall be entitled to the sum of £4. Before the existence of the present rules which were certified by the Registrar in April last there was a rule in existence by which the widow was entitled to the sum of £6.

When the defendant made an application for the money the complainant told him he was only entitled to £4 and at the same time directed him to go and get the money off his brother as he couldn't give it him. The defendant went to the brother, who in ignorance, gave him £6 and the present action is to recover the £2 overpaid.

He (Mr. Ambler) would show that that the defendant was only entitled to £4 according to the rules, which were pointed out to him. He would contend therefore that he had obtained £2 by false pretences and in the interests of the society, should ask the Bench to send the defendant for trial: – Presiding Magistrate – You mean to say the £6 was offered to him and that he should have refused it. – Mr. Ambler: He was told by a properly constituted authority that he was only entitled to £4 and went and claimed £6. – Mr. Marsh – It was not a written authority, I suppose or anything of that kind? – Mr. Ambler: – No. – Mr. Marsh: said that it would be inevitable that the defendant could not be prosecuted in that Court in the matter. He should go to the County Court, – Mr. Ambler: said if that was the opinion of the Bench, he would not proceed with the case. – The Presiding Magistrate; If it's a case at all, it's a case for the County Court. – Mr Marsh: – Then you will not proceed any further Mr. Ambler. – Mr. Ambler: – No, not after that intimation. – The case was dismissed'.[9]

---

9   The Leigh Chronicle, 29 January 1876, Leigh Local Studies, WLCT.

Misappropriation of Funds

Other friendly societies in addition to the Independent of Foresters suffered from misdemeanours by their members, including some of the smaller and less well-known societies such as the Grand Protestant Confederation Female Society of Lancashire. It is recorded that on 14 August 1869 the former secretary of the Society, Thomas Smith of Atherton, Lancashire, was arrested and charged with offences of obtaining seven different sums of £6, totalling £42, by representing that members were dead while in every one of the cases, the person allegedly dead was still living. The accused seems to have been given to drinking and to have neglected his work, and he appeared to be in a shocking state of nervousness.

The course the society decided to take was the most lenient one. They could have charged him with obtaining money by false pretences and sent him to the assizes or quarter sessions for trial, but since the law protected friendly societies as far as it could they were able to adopt an alternative course: they agreed that the money could be repaid to the Society and that, in default, he should be committed for three months with hard labour. He would also have to pay the sum of £20 by way of penalty.

Various witnesses gave evidence that the alleged deceased persons were still alive, and eventually the magistrates decided to make an order for the repayment of the sum of £42 and in default to stand committed for three months with hard labour; in addition to that they would inflict a fine of £5 and costs not exceeding 20 shillings. The accused was asked if he had anything to say in mitigation, to which he replied, 'No I have nothing to say that I know of'. His mother interceded on his behalf and offered to repay the money.[10]

Oronhyatekha and the Independent Order of Foresters

The Ancient Order of Foresters was adopted all over the world and grew enormously in the United States and Canada. Some societies broke away from the Ancient Order of Foresters and named themselves The Independent Order of Foresters. This Order eventually came to Britain and was subjected to scrutiny by the press during the late nineteenth century: in particular, *The Times* reported that many people were under the impression that the IOF was simply and solely a co-operative society for life insurance and friendly society purposes. The Times reported that the Chief Registrar

---

10   Leigh Chronicle 21 August 1869. No page identified. Leigh Local Studies, WLCT.

of Friendly Societies had written to that newspaper cautioning the public and that the prospectus issued by IOF was essentially misleading.[11]

The IOF certainly seemed to be under suspicion, and in an anonymous exposé enticingly entitled *Mysteries of the Independent Order of Foresters Unveiled*, prospective members were warned that if they joined they would '*surrender their independence to the control of Oronhyatekha, the American-Indian 'Supreme Chief' of that Order*'.[12] The exposé attacked the IOF mercilessly, quoting their prospectus and stating:

> '*Join the IOF – Because by joining you can secure £200, £400, or £600 Insurance, payable to your wife, children, or other beneficiaries, at a cost ranging from 2s. 6d. per month per £200 and upwards, according to age, which is little more than one-third the cost of ordinary Insurance Companies.*

> *Here seems a chance for the thrifty man of limited means securing £200 for his family; but having 'joined' he must not be surprised if other payments, which must of necessity be made, will increase the quoted figure by some 50% or to be told, on finding the IOF not an Insurance association, that if he wished simply to insure his life he should go to an insurance company, the IOF having 'another side' (aims, objectives, and usages) compliance with which was essentially necessary to the carrying of his insurance of that Order*'.[13]

More criticism followed, with comparisons being made with paganism and bogus rituals, the author finally posing the question of the society's actual relationship to life insurance:

> '*There may be, and no doubt are, people to whom donning a mask and dabbling in semi-pagan ceremonies and 'mysteries' may afford a charm of attractiveness, or who might consider it a 'privilege most valuable' to pose as amateur 'chaplain', burn incense, and officiate at the newfangled 'Altar of Liberty, Benevolence and Concord' in an IOF court-room. Tastes and opinions*

---

11   The report in the Times is mentioned in Anon., *Mysteries of the Independent Order of Foresters Unveiled, Or Trapped at the Altar of L.B.& C.*, (USA: Nabu Public Domain Reprints), p. 2.

12   Ibid., p. 4.

13   Ibid., p. 2.

differ, however, and it seems scarcely surprising that there are yet people of a practical turn of mind who would be disposed to consider the one tomfoolery, if nothing worse, and the other profanity, if not blasphemy. What on earth has this got to do with Life Insurance? – Directly nothing.[14]

The author then describes a court case in Dublin in 1894 between a former member of the Order, Laurence Joseph Kinsella, and a court of the IOF. Kinsella had apparently taken possession of a seal and a 'ritual', the property of the Court Eblana 2017 based in Dublin, and had refused to give them up, even though under rule 155 the trustees of the court were entitled to possession of them. Lawyers argued that, as the Order had originated in Canada, the property could not be the property of the IOF Court in Dublin. A witness, who was the General Manager of the society in London, argued that Court Eblana came under the law of England and Wales as the society was registered with the British Government.

The lawyer for the defendant questioned some of the wording in the ritual, which stated that a person seeking membership of the society was at peril of his life if he did so. It stated *'Captive Stranger, it is my duty to inform you that what you ask may involve the forfeit of your life. Are you willing to take that risk?'* The defence asked if that was part of the ritual, and the witness responded that it was. He then asked *'And then afterwards, is he not made to take a declaration or obligation?'* Mr Ennis, a solicitor who was appearing for the complainants, stated that he had not seen any. He was asked if he himself had taken an obligation and he acknowledged that he had. The defence lawyer then read the obligation:

> *'I…..of my own free will and accord, in the presence of the Supreme Ruler of the Universe and of the members of the Independent Order of Foresters here present, do most solemnly and sincerely promise and declare that I will ever conceal and never reveal any word, sign, grip, or token, or any of the secrets or private works of the Independent Order of Foresters which shall now or may hereafter be communicated to me, to anyone in the world. I will not repeat outside the courtroom (IOF courtroom) any transaction whatsoever which may take place therein which by the regulations of the order should be kept secret'.*

The prosecution argued that the defendant was no longer a member of the Court and therefore had no right to the items, but the defence claimed that he had every right to them until certain monies which he had expended were returned. The prosecution also put forward that the IOF was not a registered society and was thus an illegal combination within the meaning of the exceptions mentioned under the Friendly Societies Act, section 15. The judge, however, disagreed and an order was made for the defendant to return the ritual or pay the cost of the same. The seal was eventually handed over to a trustee of Court Eblana, but the saga of the ritual continued with the defendant Kinsella eventually paying 4s. 6d., the amount fixed by the Chief Magistrate as the value of the IOF ritual, and 10s. costs. The ritual was never returned to the IOF, and in various newspapers the IOF came under attack, one particular letter going as far as to suggest 'that the Independent Order of Foresters is such an association as no Catholic should have anything whatever to do with'.[15] The exposé then proceeded to reveal the ritual of the IOF.

The IOF has a three-level governing structure. Just as Freemasonry has lodges, so the Foresters have local courts. Like the Freemasons of lodges, the IOF members vote to elect their own court officers who meet on a regular basis to handle the business and the running of the court. At the second level there are the High Courts, which provide the leadership and direction to assist local courts in their activities. High Court officers are elected representatives of the courts within their jurisdiction. At the top of the IOF is the Supreme Court. This body governs the IOF and convenes every four years to elect the Supreme Chief Ranger and other Supreme Court Officers. As a Friendly Society, the IOF is operated solely for the benefit of its members and their families, providing cover for sickness and burial.[16]

During the closing decades of the nineteenth century the undisputed leader and the person credited with the incredible success of the IOF was a Mohawk from Brantford, Canada, called Oronhyatekha. Born in 1841, Oronhyatekha, which means 'Burning Sky', came to prominence amongst his people after giving a spirited speech to the visiting Prince of Wales. The Prince supposedly invited him to study at Oxford,

---

15   Ibid., pp. 6-11. The case was also widely reported in such newspapers as the Evening Telegraph, 2 March 1894, and in the Evening Herald, 15 March 1894.
16   See the Ancient Order of Foresters official website:
     <http://www.forestersfriendlysociety.co.uk/about-us/history> [accessed 2 April 2013]
     and the Independent Order of Foresters official website:
     <http://www.foresters.com> [accessed 2 April 2013]

an invitation that he accepted. It was to be his time at St. Edmund Hall, Oxford, which led to the establishment of the Oronhyatekha Society at the College, a society which comprises a group of select undergraduates going out and getting drunk while dressed in typical Native American clothing.

On returning to Canada, he married the great-granddaughter of famed Mohawk Freemason Joseph Brant,[17] and studied at the University of Toronto, gaining a medical degree and subsequently opening a practice. His importance grew, as he was elected as President of the Grand Council of Canadian Chiefs in 1874. He ultimately became involved in the Independent Order of Foresters and – working against the racial prejudices of the period – became the Supreme Chief Ranger of the IOF, transforming the Order into one of the wealthiest and most successful of the

Oronhyatekha, leader of the Independent Order of Foresters.

fraternal financial institutions. His philanthropic work included founding a museum and an orphanage, and he also became a Freemason, becoming Worshipful Master of Richardson Lodge No. 136 GRC in Stouffville, Ontario in 1894.[18]

During the period of Oronhyatekha's leadership, he passionately promoted the Order, and it was claimed that the IOF distributed more than $20 million in social welfare benefits and insurance monies to over 100,000 recipients, making the IOF a leading fraternal and financial society, which specialised in assisting the poorer sections of society. Oronhyatekha's philanthropic work, his revitalisation of the IOF, and his work as a Freemason reveal a man who endeavoured to overcome racial prejudices and someone who wanted to change the world around him for the better. He died in 1907.[19]

---

17 See Harrison, Transformation of Freemasonry, pp. 186-8.

18 See the history and past Officers of Richardson Lodge No. 136 GRC on the official website: <http://www.richardsonlodge.ca/officers.htm> [accessed 2 April 2013]

19 See the Dictionary of Canadian Biography Online: <http://www.biographi.ca/009004-119.01-e.php?id_nbr=6976> [accessed 22 October 2012]

THE ODDFELLOWS

Of all the friendly societies that have existed, the Oddfellows became one of the largest and perhaps most widespread, with a presence in most towns and cities throughout the UK during the nineteenth century. The earliest surviving records date from 1748 and relate to a lodge based in London. As we have seen, the Order quickly spread throughout England but became blighted by splits and schisms. The Manchester Unity – or the Independent Order of Oddfellows – split from the Grand United Order of Oddfellows in 1810 and further splits followed, such as the Bolton Unity and the Sheffield Unity, with other breakaway bodies being formed in Derby, Norfolk and

An Oddfellows procession through Ashton-in-Makerfield, Lancashire. Taken from an unnamed newspaper cutting and digitally reproduced by the Reprographics Department at Liverpool Hope University.

Kent, to name but a few. According to Victoria Solt-Denis in her book *Discovering Friendly and Fraternal Societies: Their Badges and Regalia* another breakaway Order, the Wolverhampton Unity of Oddfellows, became redundant when it merged with the Ancient Order of Shepherds in 1876.[1] Despite these splits, the Oddfellows remained an attractive society for a working man to join and became very successful throughout the nineteenth and early twentieth centuries.[2]

The Making of an Oddfellow

The following narrative was not taken from an Oddfellows' source but from the pen of Richardson Campbell, Grand Secretary of the Independent Order of the Rechabites, the well-known Temperance Order. He got the story from an old magazine. It tells of a man who was admitted into an Oddfellows Lodge in 1832. The curiosity about the Oddfellows shown by such a high-ranking Rechabite indicates just how interested in one another the different Friendly Societies were.

> 'At the door of the lodge I was blindfolded by the outdoor guardian, who had a drawn sword, and, with mysterious knocks and whispering, after giving the password I was admitted into the Lodge-room. All was intense silence. I felt a peculiar awe pass over me; I was told to step over imaginary steps and stoop under projecting beams, etc. All at once I was startled by the howling of members and the rattling of ponderous chains; the noise subsided and I was asked what I most wanted. My conductor whispered to me 'Say light'; I did so, and my interrogator asked me if I should know the person who proposed me. I said 'Yes'. The bandage was rudely torn from my forehead and my conductor said, 'Is that him?'

> Thrusting me close to a painted transparency representing a skeleton, or as they called it, 'Old Mortality' two members dressed as priests stood beside the picture with drawn swords, who cautioned me to be very careful and discreet

---

1 See Victoria Solt-Denis, *Discovering Friendly and Fraternal Societies: Their Badges and Regalia*, (Oxford: Shire Publications, 2008), p. 94.

2 Correspondence between Paul Eyres, Provincial Corresponding Secretary, South Yorkshire and North Derbyshire, and co-author Fred Lomax, dated 20 February 2013. See the official website: <https://www.oddfellows.co.uk/> [accessed 5 October 2014]

during my initiation, when a stentorian voice from behind the picture thus addressed me:-

'Hold! Approach me not, for know that, in my presence monarchs tremble and princes kiss the dust; at my bidding the most potent armies disappear. My shadow is the pestilence and my path the whirlwind. For thee, poor mortal, pass some few years of flowering spring, with pleasant, joyous summer and sober autumn fading into age. Then pale concluding winter comes at last and shuts the scene; then shalt though be with me. But know, to the virtuous man my approach hath no terrors; to the guilty I am terrible.

> *'So when the last, the closing, hour draws nigh,*
> *'And earth recedes before thy swimming eye;*
> *'Whilst trembling on the doubtful verge of fate,*
> *'Though strain'st thy view to either state*
> *'Then may'st thou quit this transitory scene*
> *'With decent triumph and a look serene*
> *'Then may'st thou fix thine ardent hopes on high,*
> *'And having nobly lived, so nobly die'.*

The last two lines were shouted out in chorus by all the members. I was now led to the Father of the Lodge, the Warden. I was told he was very old and feeble, and he would further assist me in the ordeal of making. In my simplicity I tried to help him from his chair, being told to do so, when, to my surprise, he grasped me with Herculean strength and shook me violently, dragging me up and down the room. He ceased and asked me if the poker was ready and asked me (as he said) in confidence if I had flannel draws on. I had been told to say 'Yes'. And he announced to the Lodge that I had flannel draws on, at which a tremendous yell of satisfaction was heard throughout the Lodge. Oh it was fearful! They had a painted poker, similar to what clowns use in pantomimes. But the funniest appearance was their grotesque and ludicrous dresses and all wore burlesque masks. I was led to the Vice-Grand, who administered the obligation; then taken to the Noble Grand, who was, I afterwards found, seated on a throne, with supporters similar to Vice-Grand, splendidly attired in 'Regalia' as it was called. My conductor told me the Noble Grand was not able to see me unless I particularly wished to see him; however, one of his supporters said he would prevail upon him to see me. They accordingly drew aside the curtains which concealed him, when he appeared to be in a state of somnolency; and being asked should I liked to have him waked, of course the simple candidate said 'Yes'.

They aroused him, with which he appeared to be very indignant, but when told that a candidate stood before him for information he relaxed his anger and addressing me said he would impart the secrets of Oddfellowship to me.

He (the Noble Grand) told me we admitted no one to become an Oddfellow under the age of 21, unless the son of a worthy brother and no bailiff or bailiff's follower, telling me to be cautious who I introduced to become a member and desired me to remove from my mind any impression I might form from the evening's procedure, for in all ages past the best and wisest of men have been taken for Oddfellows. After admonishing me further he gave the grip and password. There was a short lecture given me by the Grand Master and the important ceremony was brought to a close.

Amid the mummery of that initiation there were gems of philanthropy and kind expressions towards our fellow-man interspersed, independent of the motto of the fraternity that:

> Truth ought therefore to reign on the lips,
> Love in the affections, and
> Friendship in the heart of every Oddfellow'[3]

---

3   Taken from Campbell, *History of the Rechabite Order*, pp. 5-7.

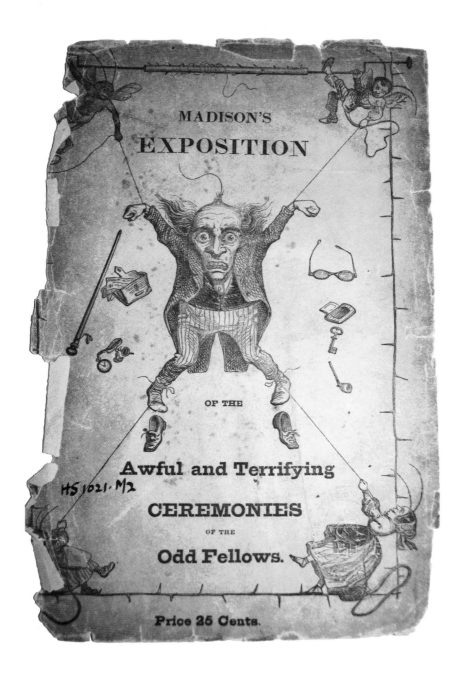

ABOVE: The three Principals' chairs in the Oddfellows lodge room in Rotherham.

LEFT: The cover of James M. Madison's 1848 'Exposition of the forms and usage observed in the various lodges of the Independent Order of Odd Fellows: as organized in the United States; together with a full account of the awful and terrifying ceremonies attendant upon the initiation of a new member into the order'.

RIGHT: The Provincial Grand Master chain and apron, held at the Oddfellows lodge in Rotherham.

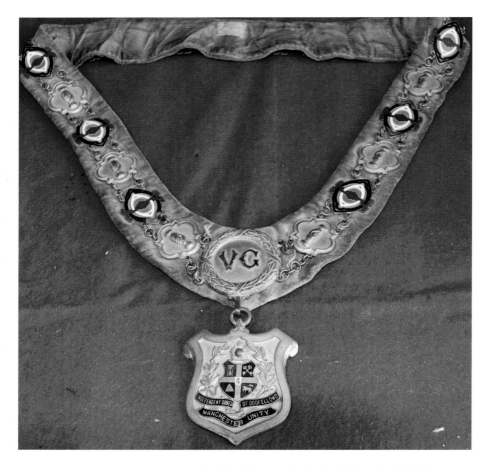

ABOVE: The Vice Grand's chain, held at the Oddfellows lodge in Rotherham.

RIGHT: The board showing the Provincial Grand Masters of the South Yorkshire and North Derbyshire District of the Independent Order of Oddfellows Manchester Unity, from 1826. *(Courtesy of the Rotherham Branch of Oddfellows)*

INDEPENDENT ORDER OF ODDFELLOWS MANCHESTER UNITY
PROVINCIAL GRAND MASTERS OF SOUTH YORKSHIRE & NORTH DERBYSHIRE

Sheffield District

Year	Name	Year	Name	Year	Name
1826	F. Hewgill	1882	F. Howe	1945	J. Lattin
1827	R. Holland	1884	W. Parkin	1946	J. Marshall
1828	J. Walker	1885	A. Flint	1947	J. Jarrams
1829	L. Spencer	1886	J. Morton	1948	J. Roebuck
1830	T. Law	1888	A. Ocxey	1949	E. Jennings
1831	J. Nicholson	1889	G. Whitfield	1950	F. Booth
1832	J. Bustard	1890	S. Bidgood	1951	J. Barrington
1833	E. Coldwell	1891	W. Lowe	1952	R. Adlington
1834	D. Raper	1892	R. Holland	1953	R. Lilley
1835	J. Penny	1893	C. White	1954	N. Smith
1836	J. Earl	1894	R. Goodison	1955	W. Humphries
1837	T. Hobson	1895	E. Surdall	1956	H. Frecknall
1838	W. Cooper	1896	H. Ward	1957	G. Gale
1839	W. Bremelow	1897	J. Dyson	1958	A. Hulberry
1840	J. Kenworthy	1898	E. Morton	1959	H. Merrills
1841	J. Corbridge	1900	G. Gardiner	1960	A. Adlington
1842	G. Ainley	1901	G. Jarrans	1961	M. Tomlinson
1843	R. Crossland	1902	J. Duncan	1962	A. Taylor
1844	L. Keeman	1903	J. Houliston	1963	Sis F. Frecknall
1845	L. Vickers	1905	W. Webster	1964	J. Turner
1846	J. Hulley	1906	W. Sidebottom	1965	N. Smith
1847	G. Ramsden	1907	G. Birtles	1966	Sis E. Taylor
1848	G. Ashmore	1908	G. Housley	1967	A. Adlington
1849	J. Eyre	1909	W. Morgan	1968	H. Frecknall
1850	G. Skinner	1910	T. Armitage	1969	R. Lilley
1851	J. Simpson	1911	T. Bacon	1970	I. H. Holmes
1852	J. Corbett	1912	G. Latin	1971	J. Turner
1853	J. Neild	1913	G. Fisher	1972	A. Rodgerson
1854	H. Green	1914	A. Andrew	1973	J. Gee
1855	E. Harrison	1916	A. Morton	1974	R. Cardona
1856	G. Ramsbottom	1917	A. Mappin	1976	W. Humphries
1858	J. Smith	1918	J. Noble	1977	H. Slater
1860	H. Garrison	1920	J. McAra	1978	D. Bradley
1861	J. Cox	1921	A. Siddall	1979	Sis B. Humphries
1862	T. Pexkin	1922	J. Hunt	1980	A. Adlington
1863	T. Hill	1923	A. Sweeney	1981	D. Bradley
1864	J. Mckenzie	1925	F. Scholey	1983	Sis E. Taylor
1865	J. Atkin	1926	J. Robinson	1984	J. Turner
1866	G. Hall	1927	H. Grayson	1985	W. Humphries
1867	C. Cropper	1928	D. Fox	1986	Sis B. Humphries
1869	W. Butterfield	1929	D. Pratt	1987	H. Slater
1870	G. Booth	1930	J. Pearson	1988	R. Swallow
1871	H. Outram	1931	J. Murfitt	1989	D. Bradley
1872	J. Addy	1932	R. Fox	1991	A. Adlington
1873	H. Sedgwick	1933	A. Marshall	1992	T. Renshaw
1874	H. Outram	1934	H. Southern	1993	Sis B. Humphries
1875	S. Goodrich	1935	H. Jarrows	1995	H. Slater
1876	S. Turner	1936	W. Lockwood	1996	D. Bradley
1877	W. Cuckson	1936	A. Gillott	1997	P. Eyre
1878	A. Smith	1937	J. Sweeny	1998	T. Renshaw
1879	W. Gardiner	1939	P. Gale	1999	Sis B. Humphries
1880	W. Person	1940	C. Baldock	2000	D. Bradley
1881	J. Willey			2001	N. Fletcher
				2002	J. Hawes
				2003	J. Wilson
				2004	B. Law
				2005	E. Fearn

Rotherham District

Year	Name	Year	Name	Year	Name
1862	J. Bradford	1915	A. Greaves	1970	H. Wilkin
1863	J. Longdon	1914	A. Woolman	1971	J. Wing
1864	G. Slother	1916	W. Skelton	1972	R. Dearing
1865	E. Jackson	1916	W. Eskholme	1973	G. Kidd
1866	J. Crookes	1917	G. Whittaker	1974	H. Wilkin
1867	H. Gummer	1918	A. Ogley	1975	H. Topham
1868	J. Norton	1919	A. Dixon	1976	Sis. Barraclough
1869	B. Shepherd	1920	E. Cruickshanks	1977	H. Wilkin
1870	H. Tyers	1921	A. Watson	1978	Sis. M. Johnson
1871	W. Law	1922	A. Garrison	1979	H. Topham
1872	J. Purnell	1923	H. Thompson	1980	H. Marsden
1873	E. Price	1924	E. Ball	1981	Sis. Wing
1874	R. Pinkerton	1925	E. Allison	1982	A. Lloyd
1875	R. Pinder	1926	A. Wilkinson	1983	H. Topham
1876	G. Jackson	1927	J. Dobson	1984	Sis. M. Johnson
1877	J. Taylor	1928	L. Taylor	1985	A. Lloyd
1878	W. Eskholme	1929	J. Butler	1986	J. Wing
1879	B. Tyer	1930	J. England	1987	H. Rawdin
1880	G. Howskill	1931	R. Pinder	1988	Sis. M. Rawdin
1881	A. Robinson	1932	E. Cogill	1989	Sis. J. Hindes
1882	A. Pinder	1933	A. Bell	1990	Sis. M. Johnson
1883	G. Iliston	1935	L. Payne	1991	J. Booth
1884	G. Gummer	1935	H. Jones	1992	J. Wing
1885	G. Walton	1937	J. Bell	1993	Sis. J. Hindes
1886	H. Pope	1938	H. Hammerton	1994	R. Dearing
1887	W. Abson	1939	H. Robinson	1995	J. Boyd
1888	W. Bell	1940	G. Hides	1996	G. Weastaff
1889	G. Crank	1941	J. Baker	1997	Sis. M. Rawdin
1890	C. Brettell	1942	G. Hides	1998	Sis. J. Hindes
1892	H. Rushforth	1943	H. Atton	1999	R. Copley
1893	W. Woodcock	1944	W. Beighton	2005	K. Copley
1894	S. Froggatt	1945	F. Sambrook		
1895	A. Law	1948	Sis E. Taylor		
1896	T. Swann	1946	L. Taylor		
1897	H. White	1947	E. Emerton		
1898	S. Smith	1948	H. Atton		
1899	R. Hattersley	1950	E. Carver		
1900	H. Simpson	1951	Sis. M. Hammerton		
1901	W. Gregory	1952	J. Emerton		
1902	W. Wadsworth	1953	H. Keeling		
1903	T. Easton	1954	A. Mangham		
1904	A. Dransfield	1955	H. Bates		
1905	P. Wadsworth	1956	G. Thompson		
1906	J. Norton	1957	R. Butler		
1907	J. Axelton	1958	R. Rawdin		
1908	S. Smith	1959	J. Thompson		
1909	S. Godber	1960	L. Troubridge		
1911	B. Bennett	1961	L. Baker		
1912	D. Butler	1961	Sis. M. Frost		
		1963	Sis. M. Hammerton		
		1964	E. Baker		
		1965	J. Gelder		
		1966	E. Troubridge		
		1968	G. Kidd		
		1969	R. Sambrook		

South Yorkshire & North Derbyshire District

2006	Sis P. Evans
2008	Sis W. Skelton
2009	M. Nicholls
2010	M. Kirby
2011	Sis E. Kirby
2012	P. Wilson

ABOVE: A ceremonial axe revealing the Skull and Crossed Bones. Similarities with the symbolism used in Freemasonry are certainly evident. *Courtesy of the Rotherham Branch of Oddfellows)*

RIGHT: The Owl, used as a symbol of wisdom within the Oddfellows lodge. *(Courtesy of the Rotherham Branch of Oddfellows)*

The initiation ceremonial banner, again revealing the Skull and Crossed Bones.

(Courtesy of the Rotherham Branch of Oddfellows)

The Treasurer's staff, revealing the Crossed Keys,
and the Hourglass, two powerful symbols also seen in Freemasonry.

(*Courtesy of the Rotherham Branch of Oddfellows*)

A banner for the Bury and Haslingden District of the Independent
Order of Oddfellows Manchester Unity, revealing the All-seeing Eye above.
(Courtesy of the Rotherham Branch of Oddfellows)

Another banner showing the All-seeing Eye set above the emblems of the Oddfellows.

(Courtesy of the Rotherham Branch of Oddfellows)

The Oddfellows in St Helens and Halebank

It is best to view the development and workings of the Oddfellows at local level, and the industrial north-west of England can supply many examples of the 'Manchester Unity' branch of the Order. The Prince of Wales Lodge, for example, was an Oddfellows lodge, which was established in 1863: it met at the Swan pub in St. Helen's in Lancashire, and by 1894 was a thriving lodge. At the time the Swan was run by Henry Ashton, who was also a prominent member of the lodge, and a glance at the lodge's meetings throughout 1894 gives an insight into how a late nineteenth-century Oddfellows lodge was organised. It held regular monthly meetings which mixed business with pleasure: the brethren discussed the Delegates' reports, but also enjoyed musical evenings, recitals, and talks on new and fashionable subjects such as 'bicycling'. The Oddfellows certainly had to balance the friendly society aspect with the entertainment and social side of the Order, and this is what made it different from Freemasonry. It therefore had more

The Swan pub in St. Helens, location for an Oddfellows Lodge in the later nineteenth century. The landlord was Henry Ashton, a member of the lodge.

The silver-snuff box showing a swan, presented to Henry Ashton by the brethren of the lodge.

room to explore other entertaining aspects of the lodge meeting and, in doing so, appealed to a different sort of man: a working man who enjoyed socialising, education and supporting his community.

In February 1894, the Lodge presented Henry Ashton with a silver snuff-box, a keep-sake which his granddaughter still possesses to this day. Perhaps, as landlord, he had provided a service to the lodge in giving them a home and supplying them with meals and drinks, a procedure that was not too different to that obtaining within Freemasonry at this time, with some Masonic lodges meeting in pubs where the landlord was a valued member. The snuffbox interestingly features a swan and a quote from Shakespeare's 'Taming of the Shrew': '*To your pleasure humbly I subscribe*'.

By 1910, an Oddfellows Hall had been built in Parr, the success of the Order in St. Helen's requiring the construction of a more versatile building. Again, the Oddfellows were following a similar process to Freemasonry, which was itself undergoing expansion at this time, with many towns witnessing the building of all-purpose Masonic Halls. The imposing Oddfellows Hall was a landmark in Parr, and was

Oddfellows pub in Parr, near St Helens, now derelict. *(Photograph by David Harrison)*

surrounded by rows of terraced houses, which housed the working men of the area. This Hall would act as a centre for the Oddfellows of the town: it was a place to discuss the financial aspects of the society, a place for entertainment, and a focal point for the families of the members. The popularity of the Order in Parr could also be seen in a pub called 'the Oddfellows' which was situated further down the same road.

Similarly, in 1924, an Oddfellows Hall was constructed in Halebank near Widnes. Once again, this was the most prominent building in the small town, with the Hall being an obvious focal point for members and their families. Both of these Halls were under the Manchester Unity branch of the Oddfellows, and at Halebank the commemorative stone indicates that the Hall housed the *'Ireland Blackburne Lodge 1801 MU'*, the Ireland Blackburne family being local gentry.

It is interesting that, by the 1970s, both these Halls had been transformed into social clubs. Gone were the meetings, the regalia, the poetry recitals and the papers on 'bicycling'; instead the Halls offered a social club for local nights out, a game of pool, a pub singer and a cheap pint. This social aspect of the society can be seen in other industrial town such as Wigan which, in the early 1980s, had a local football team called the 'Oddfellows', named after a pub.[4] The 'Oddies' – as both of the Hall's became known – were indeed part of the reason for the adaptation of the buildings. The Halebank 'Oddies' is still functioning and is still popular with the local people as a social club, but sadly the 'Oddies' in Parr closed down a number of years ago and was recently demolished.

Like many of the friendly societies discussed, the Oddfellows suffered a loss of membership after World War II, although it still survives as both a fraternal society and as a financial service provider, the total current membership being 220,000. The fraternal side only includes 65,000 of that total, and is sadly in decline. Lodges still meet, and since 1898, the society has officially accepted women members; all lodges are now mixed.[5]

TOP LEFT: Oddfellows Hall in Parr, near St. Helens, just before it was demolished. It had become known as the 'Oddies', a social club which offered a cheap pint and, at weekends, a local pub singer.

BOTTOM LEFT: Another photo of the Oddfellows Hall in Parr showing emblems on the frieze.

4   Newspaper cuttings from the Wigan Chronicle, dated from 1979-1983. Private collection. Not Listed.
5   Correspondence between Paul Eyres and Fred Lomax.

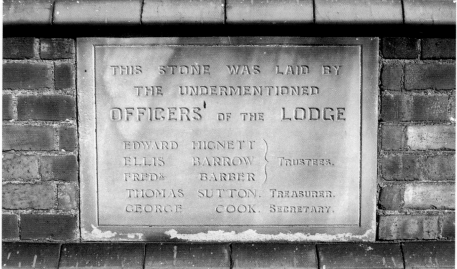

The Oddfellows Hall in Halebank, near Widnes. It is still open and the main part of the building is still a social club called the 'Oddies'. *(Photographs by David Harrison)*

THE FREE GARDENERS

This rather obscure friendly society may have existed in Scotland since the latter part of the 17th century. Some working gardeners started to protect themselves in time of need by regulating their profession, the main aim being the provision of benefits for their members. In England, there were the Trade Guilds, whereas in Scotland the crafts and trades were 'incorporated' by the Burgh councils and received a 'Seal of Cause' or Charter in order for them to control the respective trades, an example being 'The Seven Incorporated Trades of Aberdeen'.[1] These trades included the Baxters, Hammermen, Wrights and Coopers, Tailors, Shoemakers, Weavers and Fleshers.[2]

The society was originally formed in the county of East Lothian as the Gairdeners (sic) of East Lothian. The society has a minute book dating back to 16 August 1676 in which fifteen regulations for the keeping of good order are recorded. A 'Box' is also mentioned which, as we can see from many other friendly and fraternal societies, was an extremely important feature as it ensured the security of the monies belonging to the society. These early regulations also governed attendance of members, behaviour and the honour of the society. Haddington in East Lothian appears to be the town in which it was centred during its early days.

Formal gardens were a feature of many stately homes during the eighteenth century, and as these increased in number so did the number of gardeners required to look after them. It is possible that this increase led to the formation of the Order of the Free Gardeners in Scotland: certainly the area around Haddington had a good number of country-houses. Eventually, when non-working 'gardeners' were admitted to the society they outnumbered the working ones and became known as 'free-gardeners'.

We have written evidence of Lodges being formed to promote, regulate and support the craft of gardening and the gardeners themselves. The records of the gardeners of

1   Robert Cooper, *An introduction to the origins and History of the Order of the Free Gardeners*, p. 4.
2   See Ebenezer Bain, *Merchant and Craft Guilds: A History of the Aberdeen Incorporated Trades*, (Aberdeen: Edmond, 1887). For a detailed history see also <www.seventradesofaberdeen.co.uk> [accessed 30 July 2014]

Haddington and Dunfermline both survive from before 1800. They include information about gardening from a practical point of view, as well as news about plants and various gardening methods. But the early lodges had another purpose, namely to provide for their members by way of support for widows, orphans and the poor, and they therefore became benefit societies. They even provided pension rights and sickness benefit for their members, as well as annuities and grants.

In Dunfermline the Gardeners became known as the 'Ancient Society of Gardeners' and had rules concerning education, conduct, administration and control of benefits as well as entry requirements. There were however two categories of membership: professional gardeners and non-gardener members. This is very similar to early Masonic

British Order of Ancient Free Gardeners jewel.

Lodges, comprising operative working stonemasons and members of a non-operative nature. Very often in both societies the latter would be local 'gentlemen', and it was not unusual to see the names of Dukes, Earls and Lords on the members list.

But not all lodges were like that: the membership lists of some comprised gardening practitioners along with local shopkeepers, traders and members of the medical and legal professions. New lodges sought Charters from older ones and the Order began to spread: by about 1850, there were around fifty lodges. In Lancashire for instance they were quite prominent, and they even advertised the hiring-out of funeral clothing to their members, as an advertisement in the Leigh Chronicle shows.[3]

3   The Leigh Chronicle, undated newspaper cutting, Leigh Local Studies, WLCT.

'Let Brotherly Love Continue'...three jewels from the Ancient Free Gardeners.

The Order seems to have quite freely adopted some of the ritual, symbolism and regalia of Freemasonry. For instance, it is fairly well known that the Square and Compasses intertwined are a symbol of Freemasonry, and the Free Gardeners adopted the same symbols crossed with a pruning knife. They also adopted the use of aprons with elaborate designs, as well as collars and sashes, the latter used more by Scottish Masons than their English counterparts. The aprons however, were quite large and covered the chest as well as the abdomen.

The Lodge officers were the Master, two Wardens, a Chaplain and Inside and Outside Tylers. There were three degrees: Apprentice (based on Adam in the Garden of Eden), Journeyman (based on Noah's Ark), and Master Gardener (based on King

Solomon). Each ceremony included an obligation, passwords, signs and a catechism. As the Order grew various names were adopted, and by 1849 a Grand Lodge in England – The British Order of Free Gardeners – had existed for a short while. Moves were then made to set up a Grand Lodge in Edinburgh. Five lodges joined forces to form The Ancient Order of Free Gardeners, but an internal dispute led to the formation of yet another Grand Lodge, this time The West of Scotland Grand Lodge of the Ancient Order of Free Gardeners, but this did not survive.

Friendly societies changed as a result of the National Insurance Acts: many were too small to be effective, and many folded and disappeared. Some joined forces and were able to survive, and in Scotland, many became members of the Ancient Order of Free Gardeners (Scotland) National Insurance Association. But not all agreed with the terms of the Association, and some joined the British Order of Free Gardeners. It appears that the friendly society aspect of many lodges was kept separate from the fraternal side. This was also common in England where, even today, one can join the friendly society without being a member of the fraternal aspect. The introduction of the National Health Service however led to a decline in membership and many lodges closed.

The early Free Gardeners lodges used symbolism taken directly from the gardening trade: plants, and working tools such as spades, gates, rakes and many others. But they also had many symbols related to Freemasonry, such as the Sun and Moon, the Ark, Pillars, the All-Seeing Eye, a rainbow and, in particular, the Square and Compasses. The ritual made reference to the original garden, the Garden of Eden. Although specially adapted to suit the story, this too was taken directly from Freemasonry and would be instantly recognisable to any Freemason.

Their regalia, whilst consisting of aprons, were very different to those of the Masonic orders, being much longer and highly decorated with a multitude of symbols, some drawn from gardening but many others relating to the Garden of Eden, including the letters P, G, H and E representing Pishon, Euphrates, Gihon and Hiddekel, the four rivers that flow through the Garden. They also used the letters ANS – Adam, Noah and Solomon – all used in Masonic ritual. As is common with Freemasonry in Scotland, they also wore sashes to indicate their rank within the Order.

So where is the Order now in the twenty-first century? During the 1800s, the Order expanded worldwide and, at one point, is believed to have had more members than Freemasonry. However, the Order went into severe decline in the UK during the 1950s

A commemorative mug from the Free Gardeners, displaying such symbolism as the Sun and the Moon, the All-seeing Eye, three columns, the Beehive, the Hourglass and the Square and Compass, all of which are associated with Freemasonry.

and became dormant. The Free Gardeners have however survived into the twenty-first century in Australia and in Africa. The Grand Lodge of Free Gardeners (Africa) was based in Cape Town, South Africa. The Grand United Order of Free Gardeners of Australasia Friendly Society Limited represented the Australian lodges. Both were affiliated to the Ancient Order. Other lodges were started in the United States, Canada and the West Indies, with varying degrees of success.[4] In 2013, a lodge was formed in London, The Hanging Gardens Lodge No. 13, which is prospering well. In Scotland, several lodges have been formed since 2002 when Adelphi Bluebell Lodge No. 4 was formed by a number of individuals wanting to re-establish the Order. There are also lodges in Ayrshire, Stirling and Aberdeenshire as well as a Free Gardeners Lodge in Virginia USA, Virginia Bluebell Lodge No 8. There is no overall Grand Lodge, and each lodge is independent.[5]

4   For a general examination of the history of Friendly Societies, see <www.historyshelf.org> [accessed 30 July 2014]

5   Correspondence between James Jack, Secretary of Adelphi Bluebell Lodge No. 4, and co-author Fred Lomax, dated 10 June 2014.

THE SOCIETY OF THE HORSEMAN'S WORD

This particular society based in Scotland and having its origins in the eighteenth century, purported to hold ancient secrets and mysteries, with its members reputed to have magical powers over both animals and women! It was initially a friendly society, but had mystical and rustic overtones, with the Horsemen, as well as (and more particularly) the Toadsmen and the Ancient Order of Bonesmen of East Anglia, being linked to witchcraft. Indeed, the Horsemen have been referred to as 'Horse Witches' and their skills at controlling horses are reminiscent of the modern-day Horse Whisperers.

With the advent of the draft horse replacing oxen for ploughing in parts of northern Scotland, men with the skill to control horses were in great demand, and these 'horsemen' bonded together to protect their pay and benefits and to warrant that the men were well trained in the art of the 'horseman's word'. This ensured that only a brother of the society would work for the farm owners, thus giving the brethren a sense of security.

The society had an initiation ceremony, oaths and secret passwords, and appeared to have been influenced by Freemasonry and the Miller's Word – another society with mystic and rustic overtones, as the Miller's word itself supposedly had the power to control the workings of a mill. The supernatural elements of these societies also enabled the brethren to exert an element of power that secured work, good wages and respect in their countryside communities, with the friendly society and the supernatural aspects working together to create a strong sense of fellowship between the men.

Of course, the secrets of the Horsemen included a basic, practical knowledge of horses, such as being aware of a horse's powerful sense of smell and their liking for treats such as sweets. Looking after the horses and treating them well was another obvious factor. The society seems to have disintegrated by the mid-twentieth century with the introduction of farm machinery, though books are still being written about the society, and there are to this day people with the skills to control horses, as people of a trained equestrian background will inform you![1]

Another similar rustic society of a supernatural nature was the Toadsmen of East Anglia. This society was similar to the Society of the Horseman's Word, although they claimed to exert power over animals and people alike by the use of a Toad's Bone ritual, which was conducted by farm-workers of the area. First a toad had to be captured and killed. Its bones would then be used in a magical ceremony which was part-divination, part-ritual. The toad bones were wrapped in cloth and then placed in a river, preferably on St. John's Night – which, of course, was a popular Masonic feasting day during the eighteenth and early nineteenth centuries. A pact with the Devil followed to enable the mysterious Horseman's Word to be acquired, and supernatural power was then bestowed upon the Toadsman. The Ancient Order of Bonesmen, again from East Anglia, were of a similar magical ilk, using magical rituals and talismans to gain power over animals – a secret magic kept within the society to give the brethren a certain supernatural power within their rural farming communities.[2]

---

1   See George Ewart Evans, *Horse Power and Magic*, (London: Faber, 1979).
2   See Nigel Pennick, *Folk-Lore of East Anglia and Adjoining Counties*, (Spiritual Arts & Crafts Publishing, 2006).

THE LOYAL ORDER
OF ANCIENT SHEPHERDS

This Order was founded in Ashton-under-Lyne in 1826 as a sick and burial club and, like the Good Templars and the IOR, was open to both men and women. It was named 'Shepherds' as it was inspired by the shepherds of the Nativity, and grew rapidly in England before spreading to Scotland by 1868, soon becoming an established 'secret society' with its own ceremonies and ritual based upon biblical events. The Order had 'lodges', 'oath'-taking and an initiation ceremony and, like the other societies examined, the members wore regalia somewhat similar to that of the Freemasons.

Christus Noster Pastor: Chain of Office of the Loyal Order of Ancient Shepherds

As previously discussed, many friendly and fraternal societies started off as 'box' clubs, usually located in a public house where men would gather for a drink. The 'box' would have three locks, and each member of the club would deposit an amount of money as required by membership of the club. The accumulated funds would be used to pay for the burial of a member or his widow and, in some cases, sickness. They were a way of lessening the burden of the poor on the rates. Access to the 'box' was again strictly controlled, with the presence of three 'officials' being required to open it – hence the three locks (see photo of the Oddfellows box). The Ancient Shepherds seemed to have developed from a similar idea, and there is evidence of sums being paid out for members.

There is a record in the Leigh Chronicle of Lancashire dated 10 March 1866 of the sum of £8 (equivalent to approximately £365 in 2015) being made available by the Ancient Shepherds for a decent interment.[1] There was also a sick fund connected with the Order, and a member was entitled to a card if he needed to travel in search of employment, so that a Shepherd would always be sure of that assistance from the various lodges he encountered on his route to keep him from starvation. At one meeting in 1866, a local lodge initiated nearly 40 persons at the same meeting with an initiation fee of 2s. 6d. each (equivalent to approximately £5.70 in today's money). Membership of the Order at the time is stated as being 80,000 nationally, with 1,212 lodges. By the following year (1867) the Order had grown again to 100,000, with 1,300 lodges under 78 Districts and a capital of two million pounds sterling.[2]

Their benevolence was not just focussed within the Order but also in the community, as shown by a newspaper report in the Wigan Observer dated 18 October, 1879 regarding the launching of the lifeboat 'Good Shepherd' at Cemlyn in North Wales to rescue a vessel stranded in thick fog. The lifeboat had been presented to the National Lifeboat Institution as a result of voluntary subscription from the members of the Ancient Shepherds.[3]

The National Insurance Act of 1911 affected the many Friendly Societies, which, not surprisingly, were against it. The purpose of the Act was to provide for the compulsory insurance of lower-paid workers, and set a fixed capitation fee for doctors. The government paid two-ninths of these fees, the remainder being made up by insurance. National Health Insurance Committees, which represented doctors, local authorities and approved societies, administered the system. However, the act only

---

1   Leigh Chronicle, 10 March 1866. Leigh Local Studies, WLCT.
2   Ibid.
3   Wigan Observer, 18 October 1879, p. 5. Wigan and Leigh Culture Trust Archives.

Collar from the Ancient Order of Shepherds

applied to wage earners: their families had to rely on the outpatient clinics of voluntary hospitals for treatment, and many were not covered at all.

On 10 March 1913, the Chief Shepherd, visiting a lodge in Lancashire, showed his concern by suggesting that the introduction of the Act had changed the circumstances of the Order and affected its influence with the public. He must have already foreseen what the effects of the Act would be, and he suggested that the lodges should concentrate on the juvenile aspect of the Order by recruiting as many young people as possible.[4]

Concerns about government legislation were nothing new: in a report from the Leigh Chronicle in August 1874 of a lodge meeting of the Ancient Shepherds based at the Royal Oak Inn, King Street, in Leigh, the prospect of the Friendly Society Act and the uncertainty it could bring was raised in an after-dinner speech. This speech, given by Past Master Cleworth, mentioned the flourishing state of the Order, and he '*hoped that all Shepherds, as well as other Orders, would be united to resist this 'Frenchified' notion of meddling with working men's clubs'.* He went on to emphasise that '*there were no policemen needed in Lodges, and he hoped they would all resist any such clause being inserted in the Friendly Societies Act'.*[5] The Friendly Society Act was passed the following year.

As with many other orders with a fraternal side to their organisation the influence of Freemasonry was not far away, especially when it came to the ceremonial aspect, as the following address demonstrates:

AN ADDRESS

To be delivered by the PM to the members and newly elected officers of the Lodge after having received their charges

Members, such is the nature of our Institution that as some must of necessity rule and teach, so others must of course learn to submit and obey. Humility in both is an essential duty. Those whom you have appointed to assist me in government of this lodge are too well acquainted with the Principles of Shepherdry and the power with which they are entrusted and you are too sensible of the propriety of their appointment and too generous disposition to

---

4   Wigan Observer, 22 March 1913 p. 3. Wigan and Leigh Culture Trust Archives.
5   Leigh Chronicle, 15 August 1874. Leigh Local Studies, WLCT.

envy their preferment. From the knowledge I have of both officers and members, I trust I shall have but one aim to please each other and unite in the grand design of communicating happiness.[6]

This speech would have been delivered at the conclusion of a ceremony, and has certain similarities to ceremonies conducted in Masonic lodges and, indeed, the other friendly societies we have discussed.

The Ancient Shepherds seem to have survived until after World War II, when their membership began to dwindle. Like so many of the societies examined, the Order evolved into a modern financial services organisation called the Shepherds Friendly Society, which has offices based in Manchester.[7]

Selection of jewels from the Loyal Order of Ancient Shepherds

---

6   Anon., *The Loyal Order of Ancient Shepherds, Ashton Unity,* (W. Paterson & Co., 1938), pp. 21-2. Obtained by kind permission from Craig Geddes, Council Records Manager, East Renfrewshire Council.

7   See the official website: <www.shepherdsfriendly.co.uk> [accessed 1 October 2014]

GENTLEMEN'S CLUBS

As the nineteenth century progressed and the working classes bonded together in the many friendly societies and trade unions, the upper classes enjoyed a different type of club – one that provided for gentlemen interested in the pursuit of pleasure. These elite gentlemen's clubs certainly offered a sense of belonging, and attracted many famous Freemasons of the time, some clubs having a certain mystery to them and featuring some ceremonial aspects. These clubs became the playground of the wealthy and the ambitious, and many were immortalised in the popular fiction of the time, Oscar Wilde for example emphasising the importance of being a member of a club in his 1891 work *Lord Arthur Savile's Crime*:

> '…I will send you a cheque to-morrow. What is your club?
> I have no club. That is to say, not just at present'.[1]

Indeed, being a member of a club was vital for an up-and-coming gentleman and, as we shall see, his club would define his political persuasions, some clubs being Tory, others being Whig. Other clubs were for Military Officers and others for Naval Officers.

As Freemasonry became an increasingly desirable social activity for industrialists and professionals in the mid-nineteenth century, other gentlemen's clubs and learned societies became part of their social lives: the dining-, gambling- and reading-rooms of the clubs and societies became places where young up-and-coming gentlemen could learn and then flaunt their newly-acquired social skills. As with many gentlemen's clubs in England there are those who are 'in', and those who are not, and for most ambitious young gentlemen who were in pursuit of networking opportunities and securing a career, it was almost certainly better to be 'in'.

The many gentlemen's clubs situated in London reflected this attitude, as many clubs were founded in the eighteenth and nineteenth centuries for various types of

---

1   Oscar Wilde, *The Complete Works*, (London: Magpie, 1993), p. 174.

gentlemen, be it for aristocratic Whig or Tory gentlemen, for travelling gentlemen, for authors and poets, or for Army and Navy Officers. Most clubs had their exclusive premises situated within private buildings of high neoclassical architectural splendour and, like Freemasonry, had strict club rules, stringent dress codes, were strictly for men only, had high subscription fees, and balloted new members. Many of these fashionable clubs were centred on the prestigious and elegant area of St James' Square and Pall Mall.

White's, Brooks's and Boodle's

Aristocratic Whig and Tory Clubs had flourished in the eighteenth century: these included White's, the oldest surviving club, established in 1693, situated on St James', which was Tory, and Brooks's, founded in 1764, which was Whig, and which was situated just down the road from White's in St. James' Street. Brooks's was just opposite Boodle's, which was another prestigious aristocratic Tory club which had been established in 1762. Notable Freemasons who were members of Boodle's included the Duke of Wellington and the historian Edward Gibbon.[2] The Whig club Brooks's was extremely exclusive and attracted many leading politicians as well as many aristocratic and Royal Masonic members, such as the Prince of Wales (later George IV) and his brothers Prince Frederick, Duke of York, who was for a time the Grand Master of the 'Antients', and Prince William, Duke of Clarence (later William IV).

Other members of Brooks's that were linked to Freemasonry were Tory Minister Charles Watkin Williams Wynn (the elder), whose family had a lodge which had operated from their family home at Wynnstay in North Wales. Charles retained his administration under Freemason George Canning and, though a Tory, also held the position of Secretary of War for a time under the Whig Lord Grey, who was one of the principal architects of the Reform Act of 1832. Other Masonic members included the Whig politician Edmund Burke and historian Edward Gibbon, who had been linked to the Whigs but was also a member of the Tory Boodle's club. Gibbon was a member of many London clubs, such as Samuel Johnson's Literary Club, and moved with ease through London society, being comfortable in both Tory or Whig clubs alike. Burke was also a member of Johnson's Literary Club, along with Freemasons James Boswell

---

2   F.H.W. Sheppard (General Editor), 'St. James's Street, East Side', in *Survey of London: volumes 29 and 30: St James Westminster, Part 1* (1960), pp. 433-458. <http://www.british-history.ac.uk/report. aspx?compid=40621> [accessed 16 April 2009]

and Joseph Banks. Brooks's was famous for its gaming-room where a member could gamble throughout the day and night in the company of his like-minded friends, the club being a gentlemen's 'refuge', not only from their Creditors, but also from their wives and the many mistresses they might have.

The Travellers Club

Other exclusive clubs began to appear in London, such as The Travellers Club which was founded in 1819 specifically for gentlemen that had travelled at least five hundred miles in a direct line from London. The current building housing The Travellers Club on Pall Mall was built in 1832 by the architect Sir Charles Barry, and was based on Raphael's Palazzo Pandolfini in Florence, which Barry had encountered during his recent Grand Tour. The club library is extensive and decorated with a cast of the Bassae Frieze, which were originally reliefs from the Temple of Apollo discovered by architect and founder member Charles Robert Cockerell, who had assisted Freemason Robert Smirke in rebuilding the Covent Garden Theatre. Freemasons the Duke of Wellington and George Canning were both members, and the club's membership later became linked to Foreign Office officials.[3]

The rules of balloting for members of the Travellers Club were discussed by Charles Dickens Jnr. in *Dickens's Dictionary of London* of 1879:

> '*The members elect by ballot. When 12 and under 18 members ballot, one black ball, if repeated, shall exclude; if 18 and upwards ballot, two black balls exclude, and the ballot cannot be repeated. The presence of 12 members is necessary for a ballot*.'[4]

Balloting of course, was an important feature of friendly societies and Freemasonry, but other similarities were apparent, such as certain moralistic rules which were evident in some of the gentlemen's clubs, like the ones described by Peter Cunningham in his *Hand-Book of London*, published in 1850:

---

3   See the official website for the Travellers Club <http://www.thetravellersclub.org.uk> [accessed 16 April 2009]

4   See Charles Dickens Jr, *Dictionary Of London: An Unconventional Handbook*, (London: Charles Dickens and Evans, 1879).

'*That no dice and no game of hazard be allowed in the rooms of the Club, nor any higher stake than guinea points, and that no cards be introduced before dinner*'.[5]

Canning was also a member of other clubs, dining frequently at White's, on which he commented in his journal after a visit in February 1795:

'*In the evening we went to White's, which was more brilliant tonight than I have ever yet seen it. The faro table was open for the first time that I remember since I have been in the habit of going there*'.[6]

He also frequented the Crown and Anchor Law Club, regarding which he mentioned the introduction of a fine for absent members:

'*They have just passed a law, inflicting upon every member, who is in town, and who fails attending for a whole week, a fine of 5 shillings. So I went and dined at my own expense out of pure economy to save the fine*'.[7]

For a young up-and-coming MP like Canning, being a member of influential clubs such as White's would certainly help him in forming connections in London, and his references to them in his journal provide an insight into how popular and essential they were. When Canning became a Freemason in 1810, he joined two of the most prestigious lodges in London: Lodge No. 4, which was one of the four original lodges that had formed the 'Premier/Modern' Grand Lodge of 1717, and the Prince of Wales Lodge No. 259, the membership of which included the Prince of Wales himself.

The Army and Navy Club

The Duke of Wellington was also a patron of the Army and Navy Club, which was originally founded as a Commissioned Officers Army Club in 1837. However, when Wellington was initially asked to be a patron he refused unless membership was also

---

5   Peter Cunningham, *Hand-Book of London, past and present*, (London: J. Murray, 1850), p. 511.

6   P. Jupp, (ed.), *The Letter-Journal of George Canning, 1793-1795*, Royal Historical Society, Camden Fourth Series, Volume 41, (London, 1991), p. 214 and p. 281.

7   Ibid., p. 120.

opened up to commissioned officers from the Royal Marines and Royal Navy. This was agreed to and the club duly opened in St James' Square. A new club building was opened on Pall Mall and the corner of George Street in 1851, specially designed by C.O. Parnell and Alfred Smith and influenced by the Palazzo Corner della ca' Grande in Venice. The foundation stone was laid on 6 May 1848 by the chairman of the committee of management Lieutenant Colonel H. Daniell, though without the lavishness and ritual of a Masonic foundation stone-laying ceremony. Wellington was President of the club from 1838-1841. Prince Adolphus, the Duke of Cambridge, was President from 1845-1850 although, unlike his six brothers, he did not become a member of the Craft.[8]

It would have been prestigious for any club to obtain the membership of Wellington after his success at Waterloo. He was the epitome of the English war hero, and though his Masonic career was brief and had taken place in his younger years he would have recognised the value of becoming a member of an influential London gentlemen's club and would have been familiar with their traditions, etiquette and conventions. Wellington was, however, suspicious of the radical clubs, and in later life somewhat distanced himself from Freemasonry, and never attended a lodge again after 1795.

Crockfords

Wellington also sponsored William Crockford in founding Crockfords, the famous gaming club in 1828, of which the gambler, Waterloo veteran and society gentleman Captain R.H. Gronow once said:

> '...the most agreeable conversation, the most interesting anecdotes, interspersed with grave political discussions and acute logical reasoning on every conceivable subject, proceeded from the soldiers, scholars, statesmen, poets, and men of pleasure, who, when the 'house was up' and balls and parties at an end, delighted to finish their evening with a little supper and a good deal of hazard at old Crockey's'.[9]

Crockfords certainly seemed to be a very agreeable club, attracting society gentlemen

8   See the official website for the Army and Navy Club <http://www.armynavyclub.co.uk/the-club/index. php> [accessed 16 April 2009]

9   Captain R.H. Gronow, *Celebrities of London and Paris*, (London: Smith, Elder & Co., 1865), p. 104-5.

like Gronow, who, writing in 1864, noted an already stark difference in the social make-up from his time:

> 'The tone of the club was excellent. A most gentlemanlike feeling prevailed, and none of the rudeness, familiarity, and ill-breeding which disgrace some of the minor clubs of the present day'.[10]

Indeed, Gronow noted how the class of the clubs had changed since the early nineteenth century:

> 'In 1814 ... the members of the clubs in London, many years since, were persons, almost without exception, belonging exclusively to the aristocratic world. 'My tradesmen', as King Allen used to call the bankers and the merchants, had not then invaded White's, Boodle's, Brooks's, or Watier's. White's was decidedly the most difficult of entry; its list of members comprised nearly all the noble names of Great Britain'.[11]

These 'tradesmen', as they were referred to by Gronow and his aristocratic associates, would become the burgeoning middle class, intent on gaining access to gentlemen's clubs and Freemasonry in the latter half of the nineteenth century, infiltrating them with the desire to mix with the aristocracy, to network and to ultimately improve their social status. As a member of the select group of aristocratic society gentlemen who dominated the club scene in the early nineteenth century – people like Count d'Orsay and Beau Brummell – Gronow was obviously angered by this infiltration by the up-and-coming middle classes.

The Reform Club

The 'mystery' and 'aesthetic' of the London gentlemen clubs included the essential exclusive dining-room, library, coffee-, morning- or smoking-rooms, and the games-room, all intended to encourage the creative and stimulating conversation of

---

10 Ibid., p. 105.
11 Captain R.H. Gronow, *Reminiscences of Captain Gronow*, (London: Smith, Elder & Co., 1862), p. 76.

like-minded gentlemen. Disagreements and trends in progressive thought did however lead to the formation of new clubs, such as the Reform Club, which was founded in 1836 by the new Liberal supporters of the Reform Act of 1832. It was formed as a result of the older Whig Brooks's Club being unwilling to admit a large number of new members. The building, like the nearby Travellers Club, was designed by Sir Charles Barry in 1841 and was influenced by the Farnese Palace in Rome. Masonic members included Winston Churchill and Sir Arthur Conan Doyle, as well as Liberal Prime Minister William Ewart Gladstone who, though not a Freemason, came from a family with Masonic associations.[12] The Reform Club was one of the first clubs to offer bedrooms to its members, a feature that became essential to most of the London gentlemen's clubs in their endeavour to cater for out-of-town members.[13]

The Athenaeum Club

The Athenaeum Club was another highly influential club with an equally influential membership list. Throughout the nineteenth and early twentieth century it had many Freemasons as members, such as the Duke of Wellington, Rudyard Kipling, Sir Walter Scott, Sir Arthur Conan Doyle and Winston Churchill. It was founded in 1824 for gentlemen involved in scientific, literary and artistic pursuits and those involved in public service and, as a result, included what appeared to be the intelligentsia of the London social scene. The club building was designed in a neoclassical style with friezes copied from the Parthenon, and like the other Pall Mall establishments reflected the aesthetic of a London gentlemen's club. Other notable members during the nineteenth century were Charles Dickens and Charles Darwin.[14]

The Royal Institute of British Architects was similarly founded on the principles of promoting and celebrating British architecture, and brought together like-minded

---

12 William Ewart Gladstone's elder brother Robertson Gladstone was an influential Freemason in his home-town of Liverpool, being a member of the Ancient Union Lodge No. 203. The Prime Minister was named after William Ewart, a close friend and associate of his father John Gladstone, Ewart being a member of the Merchant Lodge No. 428 in Liverpool.

13 See the official website for the Reform Club <http://www.reformclub.com> [accessed 16 April 2009]. See also F.H.W. Sheppard (General Editor), 'Pall Mall, South Side, Existing Buildings: The Reform Club', *Survey of London: volumes 29 and 30: St James Westminster, Part 1* (1960), pp. 408-415, <http://www.british-history.ac.uk/report.aspx?compid=40611> [accessed 16 April 2009]

14 Archives in London, The Athenaeum, Ref: GB 1969, <http://www.aim25.aac.uk/cgi-bin/search2?coll_id=7253&inst_id=87> [accessed 16 April 2009]. See also the official website for The Athenaeum Club, <http://www.athenaeumclub.co.uk/> [accessed 16 April 2009]

gentlemen. Formed ten years after the Athenaeum Club as the Institute of British Architects in London, it was granted a Royal Charter in 1837 under Freemason William IV, and after dropping 'London' from the title moved in 1934 to its current location in Portland Place. One of its original founders was architect Thomas de Grey, 2nd Earl de Grey, whose nephew, George Robinson, Earl de Grey and Ripon, was Grand Master of the UGLE from 1870-1874. Thomas de Grey was the first president of the Institute, besides being a Fellow of the Royal Society and the Society of Antiquaries.[15]

University Clubs

Universities also had clubs for the sons of gentlemen, such as at Oxford University where the infamous Bullingdon Club was formed. Famed for its riotous and rowdy behaviour, the club became an exclusive and rather secretive dining club for undergraduates in the later nineteenth century, catering mainly for Royalty and the sons of the aristocracy. Brethren of the Oxford-based Apollo University Lodge who were also members of the club included Prince Albert Edward and Cecil Rhodes. More recently, British Prime Minister David Cameron and fellow Conservative politicians such as George Osborne and Boris Johnson were members. In the USA, Fraternal Societies linked to Universities such as the Order of Skull and Bones became popular. Founded at Yale University in 1832 for undergraduates, the Skull and Bones, which has obvious Masonic overtones has, over the years, attracted such well-connected 'Bonesmen' as US Presidents George Bush and his son George W. Bush, and US Secretary of State John Kerry. The Order has admitted female undergraduates since the early 1990s.

---

15   Thomas Philip de Grey, <www.oxforddnb.com> [accessed 2 November 2014]

Entrance to the RIBA, London. *(Photograph by David Harrison)*

FREEMASONRY, OCCULT SOCIETIES, AND THE VICTORIAN SEARCH FOR HIDDEN KNOWLEDGE

The networking that took place in the London gentlemen's clubs stimulated the vivid imagination of Victorian writers, some of whom had even experienced the mysterious activities that occurred behind the clubs' closed doors. Writer and Freemason Sir Arthur Conan Doyle[1] made a literary reference to a London gentlemen's club in his 1893 Sherlock Holmes short story *The Adventure of the Greek Interpreter*, where Sherlock Holmes visits his brother Mycroft at the mysterious 'Diogenes Club' which he describes as:

> *'the queerest club in London' being for gentlemen 'who have no wish for the company of their fellows. Yet they are not averse to comfortable chairs and the latest periodicals'.*

The bizarre rules of the club are described:

> *'No member is permitted to take the least notice of any other one. Save in the Strangers' Room, no talking is, under any circumstances, permitted, and three offences, if brought to the notice of the committee, render the talker liable to expulsion. My brother (Mycroft) was one of the founders, and I have myself found it a very soothing atmosphere'.*

The location of the club in the story was given as being on Pall Mall, a short distance from the Carlton Club, Conan Doyle describing its interior as having a games-room

---

1   Sir Arthur Conan Doyle was initiated into the Phoenix Lodge, No. 257, at Southsea, Hampshire, on 26 January, 1887.

and *'a large and luxurious'* reading-room. The 'Diogenes Club' was fictional, but given Mycroft's secretive role within the British government, the club was presented as having possible deeper mysterious political agendas.[2] Unlike the 'Diogenes Club', the Carlton Club was very real, and was yet another Tory club, which was formed in the wake of the Reform Act of 1832. William Ewart Gladstone had joined as a young aspiring politician, but resigned as his political persuasions became more liberal.[3] Conan Doyle was obviously inspired by the secrecy and mysterious nature of such Gentlemen's Clubs, so it is not surprising that he also occasionally referred to Freemasonry in his Sherlock Holmes stories, such as in *The Red-Headed League*, when Holmes – who was obviously very familiar with Masonic symbolism – recognised that someone was a Freemason, the gentleman in question being surprised that Holmes knew of his membership:

> *'I won't insult your intelligence by telling you how I read that, especially as, rather against the strict rules of your order, you use an arc and compass breastpin'.*[4]

The Authors' Club

Sir Arthur Conan Doyle, along with fellow Freemasons Rudyard Kipling, Henry Rider Haggard and Jerome K. Jerome, wrote letters of goodwill when the Authors' Lodge No. 3456 was consecrated in November 1910, the lodge having a direct connection to the London-based Authors' Club, which had been founded in 1891. The lodge was constituted by the Masonic members of the Authors' Club, one of the founders being Masonic historian A.F. Calvert, who had famously discovered an early Masonic *Catechism* dating from the early eighteenth century, which he eventually sold to Masonic historian Douglas Knoop.[5] The consecration of the Authors' Lodge reveals the intricate relationships between certain gentlemen's clubs and Freemasonry, the founding of the

2   Sir Arthur Conan Doyle, *The Adventure of the Greek Interpreter*, in *The Adventures of Sherlock Holmes*, (Herefordshire: Wordsworth Editions Limited, 1992), pp. 399-401.

3   Philip Magnus, *Gladstone A Biography*, (New York, E.P Dutton & Co., 1954), p. 146.

4   See Sir Arthur Conan Doyle, *The Adventure of the Red-headed League*, in *The Adventures of Sherlock Holmes*, (Herefordshire: Wordsworth Editions Limited, 1992), p. 133. Conan Doyle also referred to Freemasonry in other Sherlock Holmes stories, such as *The Adventure of the Norwood Builder* and *The Adventure of the Retired Colourman*, as well as mentioning Freemasonry in his other works.

5   *Authors' Lodge Transactions iii*, (London, 1919), p. 408.

lodge being seen not only as a way of promoting the Authors' Club amongst Freemasons but also of providing a means of promoting Freemasonry within the club, as attracting literary men into the Craft '*could not fail to add lustre to the Order*'.[6]

Kipling and Rider Haggard were very close friends, and both discuss Freemasonry quite openly in their writings. Indeed, Masonic themes can be seen in Rider Haggard's late Victorian works *King Solomon's Mines*, *The Holy Flower*, and the wonderfully exotic novel *She*, a story which deals with death and re-birth.[7] These works present the idea of the heroic explorer searching in lost civilisations for hidden knowledge and, along with Kipling's *The Man Who Would Be King*, testify not only to the popularity of Freemasonry at the time but also to the acceptance of the Craft in Victorian society which, within these literary contexts, also conveyed an element of mystery and the occult. Rider Haggard and Conan Doyle in particular ventured into more esoteric fields, both being linked to various clubs and Orders that dealt with aspects of esotericism and the occult: Conan Doyle was linked to the Ghost Club and Rider Haggard to the Golden Dawn.

Rider Haggard was also a close friend of the Egyptologist and occultist Ernest A. Wallis Budge. Both of them, along with Kipling, were celebrated members of the literary Savile Club.[8] Conan Doyle, like fellow-Freemason and writer Arthur Edward

---

6   *History of the Authors' Lodge No. 3456*, (London, 2000).
7   Henry Rider Haggard was initiated into the Lodge of Good Report No. 136 in 1877, but resigned in 1890. His book *King Solomon's Mines* was published in 1885, *She* in 1887, and *The Holy Flower* in 1915. See also Thomas Michael Greene, 'Clubs, secret societies and male quest romance', a PhD thesis at the University of Massachusetts Amherst, 2002, which looks at Kipling's and Rider Haggard's Masonic associations and the Masonic themes in their work. Rider Haggard's membership of the Golden Dawn is also discussed in Chris Hodapp, *Freemasonry for Dummies*, (USA: For Dummies, 2005), p. 188. Jerome K. Jerome's Masonic membership has also been discussed by certain Masonic historians: Jerome contributed a short story, 'The Prince's Quest', which was published in *Pot Pourri of Gifts Literal and Artistic* for the Scottish Masonic Benevolence in 1890. See also the essay by W. Bro. Antony Field, 'Famous Freemasons' (1994): <www.freemasons-freemasonry.com/tonyfield.html> [accessed 16 April 2009]. Kipling was initiated into Hope and Perseverance Lodge No. 782 E.C., based in Lahore, India, in 1886, and went on to become an honorary member of the Authors' Lodge.
8   E.A. Wallis Budge worked in the Egyptian section of the British Museum and collected many Egyptian artefacts for the Museum, visiting Egypt to establish contacts with dealers in Egyptian antiquities and so adding to the Museum's collection. He also wrote extensively on the history and antiquities of Egypt. He also translated the 'Book of the Dead'. Wallis Budge was keenly interested in the occult too, researching spiritualism, psychical research, reincarnation, and various hauntings. He has also been mentioned as being a member of the Golden Dawn along with Rider Haggard. His translation of the 'Book of the Dead' in 1895 certainly influenced writers and members of the Golden Dawn such as W.B. Yeats.

Waite, took a keen and almost obsessive interest in the occult, both men becoming deeply involved with psychical research. Waite also co-created the influential Rider-Waite-Smith Tarot card deck, which, when published in 1909, displayed elements of Masonic symbolism embedded within the mysterious pictures.

The Hermetic Order of the Golden Dawn and Ordo Templi Orientis

In 1891, Arthur Edward Waite had become a member of the Hermetic Order of the Golden Dawn, an occult society founded three years earlier by Freemasons Dr William Robert Woodman, Dr William Wynn Westcott and Samuel Liddell MacGregor Mathers. Waite's search for the deeper secrets of initiation led him to join Freemasonry in 1901. He became a rather prolific Masonic writer and historian who seemed to be in a constant search for the more magical origins of the Craft, writing *A New Encyclopaedia of Freemasonry* which, when published in 1921, partially reflected Waite's more mystical Masonic fancies.[9] Of his initiation, Waite commented:

> *'For myself it was a curious experience in more ways than one, and perhaps especially because it was so patent throughout that I could have told the Worshipful Master all that he was communicating to me. My Initiation was nothing therefore but a means to an end: I awaited the Grades beyond'.*[10]

Indeed, Waite was anxious to explore the more mysterious and exotic higher degrees which Freemasonry opened up to him, and by 1903 he had been accepted into various other Masonic 'Rites' and Orders, including the Rosicrucian Society of England, the Holy Royal Arch and the Knights Templar, even travelling to Scotland to receive the 'Early Grand Rite' and then on to Geneva to receive the 'Rectified Rite'. Waite was exploring all the further degrees, quenching his thirst for deeper knowledge, seeing Freemasonry as a path of mystical enlightenment. In this connection, Waite saw Masonry as very similar to the Hermetic Order of the Golden Dawn, i.e. a society that

---

9   Arthur Edward Waite was initiated into the London-based St. Marylebone Lodge No. 1305, on the 19 September 1901. See also Arthur Edward Waite, *A New Encyclopaedia of Freemasonry*, Vol. I & II, (New York: Wings Books Edition, 1996) and R.A. Gilbert, 'The Masonic Career of A.E. Waite', in *AQC*, Vol. 99, (1986).

10 See Gilbert, 'The Masonic Career of A.E. Waite', *AQC*, Vol.99. Also see Arthur Edward Waite, *Shadows of WLife and Thought. A Retrospective Review in the Form of Memoirs* (London: Selwyn and Blount, 1938), p. 162.

would endow him with the hidden secrets of Nature and Science. He saw the symbolism of Freemasonry as having the same original source as other esoteric pursuits, such as alchemy, Kabbalism and Rosicrucianism, all providing a pathway to enlightenment through the search for hidden knowledge. Waite referred to his experience by saying that:

> *'there is a Masonry which is behind Masonry and is not commonly communicated in lodges, though at the right time it is made known to the right person'.*[11]

He believed he was special enough to be accepted into the 'Masonry which is behind Masonry' – those more mysterious rituals which would only be revealed to the chosen few. He was also interested in gaining enough secret knowledge and experience to create his own rituals, Waite having plans at one stage to establish the more obscure 'Rites' in England. The Hermetic Order of the Golden Dawn certainly offered a more 'magical' experience, practising ceremonial magic and using many Masonic symbols within the ritual. The Order became extremely popular, and attracted writers and poets such as Waite, W.B. Yeats and Arthur Machen although, unlike many of the clubs and societies of the era the mysterious and magical Hermetic Order of the Golden Dawn accepted women members.[12]

The founding of the Golden Dawn can be traced back to 1887, when William Wynn Westcott, a Freemason who was constantly in search of hidden knowledge and had joined many Orders and Rites such as the Rosicrucian Society of England, obtained a mysterious manuscript in cipher from fellow-Freemason the Rev. A.F.A. Woodford. After decipherment, it turned out to be a series of rituals, and Westcott asked fellow-Freemason and Rosicrucian Samuel Liddell MacGregor Mathers to work on and expand these. Amongst the papers of the cipher manuscript that Westcott had received from Woodford, he had found the name of a certain Fräulein Anna Sprengel, a Rosicrucian adept from Germany. After writing to her, Westcott was 'granted permission' to form an English version of the Golden Dawn.

The occult Order needed three Chiefs, so Westcott and Mathers brought on board

---

11 See Gilbert, 'The Masonic Career of A.E. Waite', *AQC*, Vol.99.
12 See Mary K. Greer, *Women of the Golden Dawn; Rebels and Priestesses*, (Rochester, Vermont: Park Street Press, 1995).

fellow-Freemason Dr William Robert Woodman, who was at the time the Supreme Magus of the Rosicrucian Society of England. Thus, the Hermetic Order of the Golden Dawn was founded. Westcott even invited the elderly leader of the Southern Jurisdiction of the Scottish Rite, Albert Pike, to join, but he declined. Nevertheless, the Golden Dawn became exceedingly fashionable, attracting the likes of Waite and Yeats and, by 1896, there were five Temples and over three hundred members, and a Second Order was also thriving. Despite this success, there was disruption as the leaders began to fall out after Woodman's death in 1891: Westcott resigned in 1897 after his work in the magical Order conflicted with his career as Coroner, and Mathers also subsequently alleged that the papers that had led to the founding of the society had been forged.[13]

The Victorian interest in the occult and the search for lost ancient knowledge was fuelled by many sources, such as developments in archaeology – especially in Egypt – which were capturing the imaginations of many intellectuals at the time. The founding of the Egypt Exploration Fund in 1882 and an array of widely-available publications on Egypt, such as Amelia Edwards' *A Thousand Miles up the Nile* in 1877,[14] all helped to stir interest in the lost civilisations of Egypt and, of course, in the hidden secrets of the ancients. Before that, in 1852 the occultist, Rosicrucian and Freemason Kenneth Mackenzie – most famous for his *Royal Masonic Cyclopaedia* which was published in six parts between 1875-77 – had edited and translated *Discoveries in Egypt, Ethiopia, and the Peninsula of Sinai* by the German Egyptologist K.R. Lepsius. Mackenzie claimed to have secret knowledge of obscure Orders and rituals, most notably the 'Hermetic Order of Egypt' and the 'Order of Ishmael', the latter of which was ruled by Three Chiefs, which of course was very reminiscent of the Hermetic Order of the Golden Dawn. Indeed Waite, writing in his *Shadows of Life and Thought*, suggested that Mackenzie may have been behind the Golden Dawn ciphers.[15]

---

13 R.A. Gilbert, 'William Wynn Westcott and the Esoteric School of Masonic Research', in *AQC,* Vol. 100, (1987), pp. 6-20.

14 See Amelia Edwards, *A Thousand Miles up the Nile,* (London: George Routledge and Sons, 1891). Amelia Edwards was the co-founder of the Egypt Exploration Fund. For a further insight into the late Victorian obsession with Egyptian archaeology, see Ernest A. Wallis Budge, *The Mummy, Funeral Rites & Customs in Ancient Egypt,* (Guernsey: Senate Press, 1995), which was first published in 1893.

15 Kenneth Mackenzie, *The Royal Masonic Cyclopaedia,* (Worcester: The Aquarian Press, 1987), pp. vi-ix, in which John Hamill and R.A. Gilbert discuss Mackenzie's life and work in their 'Introduction' to the edition. Waite had put forward that Mackenzie may have partly invented the mysterious cipher, and partly been inspired by his translation of '*German Grade experiences*'; Hamill and Gilbert support Waite's claims, pointing out that Mackenzie had translated manuscripts on magic and astronomy.

Masonic interest in Egyptian mysteries was nothing new: as early as the eighteenth century certain Freemasons, such as the infamous occultist and alchemist Count Cagliostro, were claiming to possess the secrets of mysterious Egyptian Rites.[16] In England, the early Masonic interest in Egyptian mysteries can be seen in the naming of the London-based Egyptian Lodge No. 27 in 1811 and, as the nineteenth century progressed, occultist Freemasons such as Mackenzie and Waite vividly explored ideas of Egyptian mythology, trying to discover the lost knowledge of the ancients.[17]

As the nineteenth century progressed, Freemasonry increasingly attracted writers and poets such as Kipling, Conan Doyle and Rider Haggard. The mysterious nature of the Craft and the status it provided as a networking 'club' made it an essential element of their social scene, and presented an obvious inspiration for their work. Another Freemason and celebrated psychical researcher who, like Mackenzie and Waite, had also become involved in the Rosicrucian Society of England, was Frederick Bligh Bond, an architect and a keen student of the occult. Bligh Bond knew Conan Doyle, and they shared similar interests in psychical research, Bligh Bond having used mediums to assist him in his famed excavation of Glastonbury Abbey in Somerset which, according to Bligh Bond, led to the discovery that the Abbey had been built with sacred geometry. This rather unorthodox approach to his archaeological work eventually led to him being dismissed from the site by his employers, the Church of England.[18]

Conan Doyle had embraced psychical research after the death of his wife and several other close family members and until his death in 1930, he ardently supported spiritualism and constantly sought proof of life after death, a peculiarity which echoes writer and Freemason Mark Twain's interest in parapsychology in the USA. In 1922, Conan Doyle's book *The Coming of the Fairies* made clear his support for the infamous

---

16 See Philippa Faulks and Robert L.D. Cooper, *The Masonic Magician; The Life and Death of Count Cagliostro and his Egyptian Rite*, (London: Watkins, 2008).

17 Mackenzie, *Masonic Cyclopaedia*, pp. 185-8, and Waite, *Encyclopaedia of Freemasonry*, pp. 218-225.

18 Frederick Bligh Bond was a member of the Bristol-based St. Vincent Lodge No. 1404, being initiated on the 28 November 1889. He served as Worshipful Master of the lodge in 1894, although his membership ceased in 1914. He was a member of the Rosicrucian Society and the infamous Ghost Club, a club which also had links to Sir Arthur Conan Doyle and occultist and Egyptologist E.A. Wallis Budge. See Frederick Bligh Bond, *The Gate of Remembrance, The story of the psychological experiment which resulted in the discovery of the Edgar Chapel at Glastonbury*, (Kessinger Publishing Co., 1999). Also see Frederick Bligh Bond, *Central Somerset Gazette Illustrated Guide to Glastonbury*, (Glastonbury: Avalon Press, 1927).

Cottingley Fairies episode, in which two girls from Cottingley near Bradford in the north of England had supposedly taken five pictures of fairies.[19] Decades later the girls, then elderly women, admitted faking the photographs, but in 1922, Conan Doyle strongly supported their claims. His 1926 work *The History of Spiritualism* also lent his support to séances conducted by various psychics at the time and to their supposed spiritual materialisations.[20]

Interest in occult philosophy grew during the later Victorian period, not only amongst the literati of the period (best exemplified by Yeats and Conan Doyle), but also among the prosperous and educated who wished to explore mystical esoteric belief systems, and Freemasonry became a fascination for many because of this. An example of this is how Freemasonry stirred an interest in the occultist Aleister Crowley who, in the closing years of the nineteenth century, became involved in the Golden Dawn, joining in 1898, and going on from there to sample the hidden mysteries of Freemasonry after joining an irregular 'Scottish Rite' lodge in Mexico and the irregular Anglo-Saxon Lodge No. 343 in Paris.

Crowley later joined the *Ordo Templi Orientis* (OTO) which, like the Golden Dawn, is more of a magical Order which admits both men and women, but which displays a Masonic influence in its ritual. Crowley's closeness to Mathers added to growing tensions within the Golden Dawn, and it soon splintered into different groups, with Arthur Edward Waite becoming involved in the leadership of one particular faction.[21] The *Ordo Templi Orientis*, which was formed at the end of the nineteenth century, still survives today, attracting both men and women, and the Order still reveals its heavy Masonic influence, such as the wearing of aprons in certain degrees and the use of swords in the ceremony, while parts of the ritual and degree structure feature Masonic elements. There is an initial three-degree structure, and the symbolism used within the Order is also reminiscent of that in Freemasonry – the All-Seeing Eye being an obvious example. Crowley is still very much revered by its members, his *Book of the Law* being prescribed reading for initiates.[22]

---

19   See Arthur Conan Doyle, *The Coming of the Fairies*, (Forgotten Books, 2007).
20   See Arthur Conan Doyle, *The History of Spiritualism*, (Teddington: Echo Library, 2006).
21   Martin P. Starr, 'Aleister Crowley: Freemason!', in *AQC*, Vol. 108, (1995), pp. 150-161.
22   Many thanks to Kathryn McCone-Usher, who is a long-standing member of the OTO based in a lodge in Glastonbury, for supplying some information on the Order.

GENTLEMEN'S CLUBS AND SOCIETIES IN THE INDUSTRIAL NORTH WEST OF ENGLAND

For gentlemen residing outside London, clubs were being founded that were similar in character to the London gentlemen's clubs. An Athenaeum Club was founded in Liverpool in 1797, one of the founding members being the abolitionist William Roscoe, who also founded the Liverpool Lyceum Club. The Lyceum Club's beautiful Temple-like neoclassical building was built in Bold Street, Liverpool, by Thomas Harrison of Chester in 1800-1802. Both of these clubs, situated quite close to each other, were gentlemen's clubs, attracting the cream of Liverpool society, including many with Masonic connections, such as John Gladstone, a member of the Athenaeum Club, whose close associates George Canning and William Ewart were both prominent Freemasons. Both clubs offered a library and reading-room, the Lyceum becoming home to Liverpool's circulating library, which had been founded in 1757, a year before the aforementioned circulating library in Warrington.[1]

The Liverpool Lyceum and Athenaeum inspired Manchester's Portico Library, which was designed in a similar neoclassical style by Thomas Harrison, and opened in 1806. The Manchester Portico Library was built by the Manchester-based builder and industrialist David Bellhouse, who was also a founder of the Royal Manchester Institution and the Manchester Mechanics Institute. There is no evidence that Bellhouse was a Mason, but he certainly held ideals that were mirrored in the Craft: he was interested in architecture, promoted local education and was a leading philanthropist.

The Manchester Athenaeum followed in 1836, designed by the renowned architect Charles Barry and, like the Portico Library, was built to provide an education, not just for the professional classes but also for labouring men and women, with Charles Dickens even giving a speech in support of the Manchester Athenaeum in 1842.

---

1   The library is mentioned in W. Moss, *The Liverpool Guide*, (London, 1796), p. 96.

Manchester also had its own Reform Club, which was established in 1867 and which from 1871 was located in the prestigious Manchester thoroughfare of King Street in an extravagantly Gothic building designed by the architect Edward Salomons. King Street became the financial centre of Manchester, where many of its banks, building societies and insurance headquarters were located. In 1929, just around the corner in Bridge Street, the Manchester Masonic Hall was built.

An example of an early gentleman's dining club founded in Liverpool was the Unanimous Society, formed in 1753 by the wealthy Freemason and merchant Thomas Golightly. The Liverpool Athenaeum actually pre-dated the founding of its London namesake, but the gentlemen who were members were certainly drawn from a similar stratum of society: professional men of business and men of culture, like-minded gentlemen of a philanthropic turn who could relax within the aesthetic atmosphere and exchange thoughts and ideas. Later, prominent members with Masonic links included the 2nd Viscount Leverhulme who was president of the Athenaeum in 1930, his father, the 1st Viscount, being the influential Freemason who created Port Sunlight.

The intricate relationship between Freemasonry and gentlemen's clubs during the latter nineteenth century can be seen in the minutes of The Merchants Lodge in Liverpool, where in March 1882, three candidates were each managers of three local clubs: the Exchange, the Reform and the Liverpool. Social etiquette was vitally important for the up-and-coming gentlemen of this period, and access to Freemasonry and the many gentlemen's clubs not only became places to display these social skills but also allowed networking across the complex and elaborate 'clubbing' nexus. To become influential in the community it was essential that a sociable gentleman could interact in this 'clubbing' social scene, a scene of which Freemasonry was an essential part. Gentlemen who were in search of culture and seeking to climb the social ladder could, as in Freemasonry, find access to a club – if they knew existing members.

The Liverpool Cotton Brokers' Association, founded in 1841, was an essential part of the clubbing nexus in Liverpool, especially in the cotton trade, which was a vital part of the economy, not just for the north-west of England but for the whole of the country. In 1882, it became known as the Liverpool Cotton Association, and links with local Freemasonry were extremely close, with a lodge being connected to the Association. The President of the Association from 1940-1942, William Sinclair Scott

Hannay, had also been Provincial Grand Master for West Lancashire from 1952-1957, with members of the Hannay family having previously served as Presidents of the Association during the later nineteenth and early twentieth centuries. Hannay had joined the prestigious Liverpool-based St. George's Lodge of Harmony in 1910, a lodge which also featured a hefty number of cotton brokers. The Liverpool Cotton Association met at the Cotton Exchange, which was built in 1906, the building containing a ballroom, which was used by the members for all kinds of social events, including Masonic functions.

Like the previously discussed learned societies and gentlemen's clubs situated in the industrial north-west of England, such as Warrington, Oldham and Liverpool, which attracted the cream of the professional classes, the London gentlemen's clubs did the same, but on a much grander scale, the clubs attracting high-ranking aristocrats, leading politicians, natural philosophers, artists and writers. These included the men who were running the country and were involved in government – rich and powerful men who were well connected. The old paradigms of Whig and Tory were becoming a memory, and the staunch old political clubs of the earlier eighteenth century, such as the legendary anti-Stuart 'Calves' Head Club', were long gone.[2] Indeed, the Victorian gentlemen's clubs were far removed from the early eighteenth century Whig and Tory clubs, for example Jonathan Swift's Tory Brothers Club and the Whig Kit-Kat Club, with their sometimes hostile and overtly political divisions and ritualistic persuasions well and truly in the past. Politicians, no matter what their political background, could move through the gentlemen's social scene with ease. These clubs had no ritual, but some did retain traditional elements, be it toasting during the meal or traditional after-dinner speeches. Club rules dictated the culture of polite society, something that

---

2   Leigh Hunt, *The Town*, (Oxford: Oxford University Press, 1907), pp. 434-6. The 'Calves' Head Club met at a tavern in Suffolk Street, London during the eighteenth century, and at a meeting on 30 January (a date which commemorated the beheading of Charles I) the members apparently threw a calf's head wrapped in a napkin out of the tavern window and drank damnation to the Stuarts. However, when writing about the club, Hunt claimed that this was untrue:, though he admitted that the club was Protestant in political character, he says that the members did not throw a calf's head out of the window at all on this date, but that a Catholic-led mob had gathered outside the tavern and threatened the members of the club by surrounding the tavern and causing a riot. The riot was eventually dispersed, but an enduring myth about the club had been created. Hunt also mentions how the Tories stirred up mobs against the Whigs in London when Mug-Houses became centres for political meetings in the early eighteenth century, with political factions forming beer-drinking clubs where political songs were sung and toasts given, see Hunt, p. 410-11.

Freemasonry had promoted in the previous century, the Craft creating a neutral space uniting Whig and Tory and creating a political bridge.[3]

For a country gentlemen, there was his country lodge, which might have met at his private estate, such as the Masonic lodge of Sir Watkin Williams-Wynn at Wynnstay in North Wales. Lord de Tabley's country estate in Cheshire also hosted Masonic meetings, and a De Tabley lodge also met in the rural market-town of Frodsham in Cheshire.[4] This particular lodge, founded in 1862, had amongst its founder members Lord de Tabley, the Hon. Wilbraham Egerton M.P, and George Cornwall Legh M.P., the cream of the Cheshire gentry. The Masonic historian John Armstrong commented on the exclusive membership of the lodge when writing his *History of Freemasonry in Cheshire* in 1901:

> '*Probably no Lodge in the Province of Cheshire was ever established under more favourable circumstances…If in 1840 the rich men of the neighbourhood took little notice of Masonry, the same certainly could not be said in 1862*'.[5]

Other social networking activities for the country gentleman were the hunt, an example of which is the Cheshire Hunt, which in 1839 included various members of the Cheshire gentry who were also leading Masons, such as Lord de Tabley, Tatton Egerton and George Cornwall Legh. The list of local gentry included in the Cheshire Hunt of 1823 mentions Sir Harry Mainwaring, Bart. of Peover, a prominent local Freemason who served as Deputy Provincial Grand Master of Cheshire in 1832,[6] and a relative of the Col. Henry Mainwaring who had been made a Freemason with Elias Ashmole in 1646. The second Lord de Tabley, whose family had also married into the

---

3   Lawrence E. Klein, 'Liberty, Manners, and Politeness in Early Eighteenth-Century England', *The Historical Journal*, Vol. 32, No. 3, (September, 1989), pp. 583-605, on p. 587. Also see Lawrence Klein, 'The Third Earl of Shaftesbury and the Progress of Politeness', *Eighteenth-Century Studies*, Vol. 18, No. 2, (Winter, 1984-1985), pp. 186-214.

4   See Harrison, *Genesis of Freemasonry*, pp. 141-4.

5   Armstrong, *History of Freemasonry in Cheshire*, pp. 384-5.

6   Ibid., p. 95. See also *History of the Mainwaring Chapels in the Church of St. Laurence, Over Peover*, (Local Publication, 1972).

Mainwarings of Peover,[7] would become Provincial Grand Master of Cheshire in 1865, followed later by Allen de Tatton Egerton in 1887.[8] A painting entitled 'The Cheshire Hunt, 1839' by Henry Calvert which is on display at Tatton Park shows numerous members of the Cheshire aristocracy. Three generations of Egertons – of the leading Cheshire Masonic family – are depicted: Wilbraham Egerton 1781-1856, his son William Tatton Egerton, later 1st Baron, 1806-1883, and his grandson Wilbraham Egerton, later 2nd Baron and Earl Egerton 1832-1909.[9]

As the nineteenth century progressed, Freemasonry became an attractive social networking 'club' for gentlemen, industrialists and professionals, offering an element of exclusiveness that the 'middle classes' yearned for, providing another elitist society for them to join as it became increasingly fashionable. The promotion of education and service to their community was an important feature of the many clubs that emerged during the nineteenth and early twentieth centuries, such as the Rotary Club, reflecting the so called '*voluntary code of behaviour*' to which the middle classes adhered.[10] Other clubs, such as the gentlemen's clubs of London, were clubs of privilege, while other societies, such as the Hermetic Order of the Golden Dawn, explored the more occult interests of the educated who sought deeper hidden knowledge. They all however, provided a sense of bonding in an atmosphere of like-minded people, and provided a networking structure that was vital to their particular social scene during the nineteenth and early twentieth centuries.

---

7   Peter Leicester of Tabley (1588-1647) married Elizabeth daughter of Sir Randle Mainwaring of Peover in 1611, in *Cheshire Visitations pedigrees*. See also *History of the Mainwaring Chapels in the Church of St. Laurence, Over Peover*, (Local Publication, 1972), p. 20, in which a monument dated to 1573 records that Philip Mainwaring of Peover had married Anne, daughter of Sir Raffe Leycester.

8   See Armstrong, *History of Freemasonry in Cheshire*, pp. 186-9.

9   See Gordon Fergusson, *The Green Collars: Tarporley Hunt Club and Cheshire Hunting History*, (Quiller Press, 2001).

10 See C.R. Hewitt, *Towards My Neighbour: The Social Influence of the Rotary Club Movement in Great Britain and Ireland*, (London: Longmans, 1950), pp. 6-11, in which Hewitt argues that, in the early twentieth century, businessmen and other '*members of the middle classes*' became involved in the Rotary Movement as a means of performing a '*service to humanity*'. The Rotary Club was another activity for the 'middle classes' that promoted education and '*good citizenship*'. See also Hugh Barty-King, "*Round Table*" *The Search for Fellowship 1927-1977*, (London: Heinemann, 1977).

CONCLUSION

There were clubs and societies in Britain that served different classes for different reasons: the working classes of the industrial age needed security in the form of a burial club and protection for sickness and hardship, while the middle and upper classes wanted access to a club that could provide networking and career opportunities. Similar interests though could be seen throughout a cross-section of society. While the rustic superstitions of the agricultural workers of East Anglia led to the formation of magical societies such as the Bonesmen and Toadsmen, the more educated middle classes could join their own magical societies such as the Hermetic Order of the Golden Dawn and the OTO. Clubs and societies also offered a social outlet for men and, in the case of the IOR and a handful of other fraternal organisations, for women as well. These clubs and societies offered bonding and a sense of belonging, especially as the industrial communities were still developing at this time.

The influence of hard-working, charismatic men within these societies was essential to their development: men such as John White who worked tirelessly for the Old Mechanics; Charles Vivian, founder of the Elks; James J. Davis who so fervently revived the Moose; Oronhyatekha who led the IOF; and Arthur J. Riggs and Benjamin Franklin Howard of the 'black' Elks. These are all examples of how charismatic leadership can help to make a society strong and successful. The role of charismatic men also played a part in the many gentlemen's clubs: the presence of the Duke of Wellington, Count d'Orsay and Beau Brummell in a London club would certainly make the establishment attractive to up-and-coming young members. Freemasonry also had its share of charismatic figures, be it in individual lodges, such as Sir Gilbert Greenall in the Lodge of Lights or the likes of Michael Alexander Gage who was the leader of the Masonic rebellion that ultimately became the Wigan Grand Lodge.

In many of the fraternal orders discussed there were disputes and splits within the societies, with the Oddfellows, Druids, Foresters and Buffaloes all suffering 'schisms' which resulted in separate Orders being established, some, like the Manchester Unity of Oddfellows and the Grand Surrey Banner Section of the Buffaloes, being of a more localised character. These breakaway Orders also signify tensions within the societies: the Grand Surrey Banner Section for example seems to have separated itself, according to the Buffaloes historian M.W Payne, on the grounds that they 'were inclined to give themselves airs'.[1] These splits and schisms are certainly reflected in Freemasonry, with the examples of the 'Antients' separating themselves from what became known as the 'Modern' Grand Lodge in 1751, and with the establishment of independent or rebel Grand Lodges such as the York Grand Lodge and the Wigan Grand Lodge. It seems that Freemasonry was not alone in such unharmonious disputes.[2]

Friendly societies had been affected by government legislation since the later eighteenth century: the Rose Act, and successive Acts of Parliament, had attempted to regulate and, indeed, police them; shaping their development and making them evolve. This was something that continued. As Juan Baeza points out in his work *Restructuring the Medical Profession*, by the beginning of the twentieth century the friendly societies, through their role as providers of medical cover for members, and because of their sheer size at this point, were effectively controlling the GPs of the time, with the power to decide what work they received. This was naturally resented by the GPs, who campaigned against this system; this opposition was later a factor in the creation of the 1911 National Health Insurance Act.[3]

Indeed, the beginning of the end could be seen with the introduction of this 1911 National Health Insurance Act: all employed people between 16 and 70 earning less than £160 per year or, if they were manual labourers, regardless of earnings, had to join a government-approved society. The process was lengthy and confusing: employers had to purchase stamps at the post office, fix them to workers' contribution cards, and then deduct the contribution accordingly. The cards were returned to the worker's approved society, who then passed them to the Ministry as proof that the contributions had been paid. Accounts had to be meticulously kept and audited, and transactions monitored. The Ministry would then eventually credit the society in arrears. The newly-approved societies were 'governed by regulations' and the

---

1   Payne, *Origin & Development of the Royal Antediluvian Order of Buffaloes*, p. 143.
2   For more information on independent Masonic Grand Lodges in England see Harrison, *Liverpool Masonic Rebellion and the Wigan Grand Lodge*, and Harrison, *The York Grand Lodge*.
3   Juan Baeza, *Restructuring the Medical Profession: The Intraprofessional Relations of GPs and Hospital Consultants*, (Maidenhead: Open University Press, 2005), p. 5-6.

Oddfellows, one of the largest of the friendly societies, bemoaned that they '*had no idea that the Treasury grant would be bound up in so much red tape*'.[4]

The societies had effectively given up control to the relevant government department, and the secretaries of the various local lodges of the approved societies had their workload greatly increased by the new administrative demands. Funds that would have previously been kept by the friendly societies became financial reserves for the Treasury, and regulations were changed and tightened regularly, which led to more confusion and complications. There were also disputes between the societies and the panel doctors – who calculated the payments that each approved society could offer in additional benefits – with the Foresters claiming in 1928 that there was '*loose certification for sickness payments by panel doctors*'. It was the Foresters' High Chief Ranger who perhaps said what many of the societies felt when he stated that '*state administration...when it came to health insurance...was at best a machine without a soul*'.[5]

The ritualistic side of these Orders also suffered, especially as the focus began to shift to the 'insurance' side of the societies, and by 1945, the Labour Party was arguing that approved societies were inappropriate for the running of national insurances. They favoured a comprehensive health plan that operated at national level – cutting out the role of friendly societies. However, with the implementation of the 1946 National Insurance Act some of the leaders in the societies became obvious candidates to help implement the new scheme: for example, the Oddfellows Grand Master G.H. Barrow became one of many friendly society officials who became civil servants, advising the new system. The friendly societies of course could not compete with the Act, and many were to fall by the wayside.[6]

As the new NHS emerged, societies like the Oddfellows began to lose members: from having over a million members in 1945 they suffered a rapid decline, with 9,500 leaving in 1946 and 18,600 leaving the following year. In 1948, 35,500 left and 205 lodges closed. A similar story can be seen with the Foresters, Druids and the Ancient Shepherds.[7] Many of the societies consolidated and restructured, becoming mere 'insurance and benefit service' organisations. Recently however, there has been a small

---

4   Daniel Weinbren, 'Mutual Aid and the Big Society', in *The Big Society Debate: A New Agenda for Social Policy?* (Cheltenham: Edward Elgar Publishing, 2012), p. 63.
5   Ibid., pp. 62-67.
6   Ibid., p. 69.
7   Ibid., p. 69.

but determined revival in the ritualistic side of the Orders: the Druids,[8] the Society for the Horseman's Word[9] and the Free Gardeners[10] have re-emerged and opened lodges, while, of course, the Oddfellows, Foresters and Buffaloes, as we have seen, still survive as fraternal Orders, though their numbers have fallen somewhat since the 'golden age' of fraternal societies in the nineteenth century. Some fraternal societies are still strong in the USA, Canada, South Africa, Australia and New Zealand, all countries with a less state-subsidised health service.

David T. Beito argues in his book *From Mutual Aid to the Welfare State*: '*Mutual aid was a creature of necessity. Once this necessity ended, so, too, did the primary reason for the existence of fraternalism*'.[11] This can certainly be seen in the UK with the decline of friendly societies after the introduction of a strong National Health Service and welfare state, but some of the stronger and larger Orders did endure, although new membership decreased substantially, and lodges and Halls closed. In the US, when a welfare state was introduced for the very poor after the Great Depression, fraternalism was similarly affected, though again the stronger societies did survive, many of which, such as the Elks and the Moose, are still serving their communities and have a healthy following, with membership of the Elks estimated at a million and the Moose at 1.7 million. In contrast, Moose International in the UK is in serious decline, with only an estimated 2,200 members.[12]

Freemasonry can also be seen as existing under the umbrella of fraternalism: besides the many 'regular' Masonic Grand Lodges around the world, there are Masonic

---

8   Many thanks to Kai Hughes for supplying information on the 'Three Spires Lodge' No. 706, which is a lodge currently operating in Cheshire under the Ancient Order of Druids.

9   The recent publication of the work by Ben Fernee, et al, *The Society of the Horseman's Word*, (Hinckley: The Society of Esoteric Endeavour, 2009), created some media interest by including in the first hundred copies an envelope containing knotted hair from a horse's tail. This was – so it was claimed – the way in which prospective initiates were invited to join the society years ago. An initiated member of the present society also signed these first copies of the book.

10 Many thanks for the information supplied by the Adelphi Bluebell Lodge No. 4, which is a lodge currently operating in Scotland under the Free Gardeners. The lodge started to meet in 2002, the first Free Gardeners lodge to do so since the 1950s. See the official website: <www.adelphibluebell4.cco.uk> [accessed 1 October 2014]

11 Beito, *From Mutual Aid to the Welfare State*, p. 234.

12 For the current membership of the Elks, see Klein, p. 179. The estimated membership of Moose International in the US and UK was supplied by Roger Williams, Secretary to the Management Committee of Moose International British Headquarters. See also Beito, *From Mutual Aid to the Welfare State*, p. 234.

Orders for women and Co-Masonry.[13] Freemasonry still survives all over the globe but, as Masonic historian John Belton has argued, it has suffered problems both with recruitment and with the retention of new members over recent decades, and it is now in decline after experiencing a boom that peaked shortly after World War II. Belton argues that this decline in Freemasonry could be a result of '*increased civic disengagement*' due to greater individualism in our everyday lives.[14]

Of course, many societies now welcome women members or else have affiliated Orders for women, such as the Oddfellows, Elks and the Moose, which, since 1913, has had an affiliated Order, and the black Elks, which have the Daughters of the Improved Benevolent Protective Order of the Elks, all still operating. The inclusion of women members in these societies has made them more family-friendly, strengthened their links with the community, and provided a sense of inclusiveness that is necessary for a modern society. Gentlemen's clubs in the UK have also changed to reflect a modern society: many now admit women members, although many are still based on political party traditions and retain strict dress codes and high dining fees.

There will always be a need for fraternal clubs and societies for some men and women. A need to bond with like-minded people will always be with us, and we will always seek out people with similar interests, a similar class background, or similar religious or spiritual needs. To belong to a group, club or society gives us meaning. It gives us a sense of belonging and, sometimes, a sense of purpose. The fraternal societies discussed here also provided security in a rapidly changing world, but they also offered a sense of belonging, something that, despite the growth of civic engagement, we all still need as human beings.

---

13 There are two English Masonic Orders for women; The Order of Women Freemasons and The Honourable Fraternity of Ancient Freemasons, neither of which is formally recognised by the UGLE. There is also Co-Freemasonry, which is a Masonic Order for both men and women. In the US there are affiliated Masonic Orders for girls and women, such as the Rainbow Girls, and the Order of the Eastern Star. There have also been occasional examples of women joining 'regular' Freemasonry, such as Elizabeth Aldworth who is traditionally linked to a lodge in Cork, Ireland, in the early eighteenth century. See David Harrison, 'The First Lady Freemason', in *The Square*, September, 2014, p. 47.

14 See John Belton, 'Masonic Membership Myths Debunked', in *Heredom*, Vol. 9, (Washington DC: Scottish Rite Research Society, 2001), pp. 9-32.

Bibliography

Primary Source Material

Foresters Laws & Regulations, Warrington, 1842, Warrington Library, reference p1423.

List of Members of the Lodge of Lights No.148, Warrington, 1765-1981, Warrington Masonic Hall. Not listed.

List of the Members of Lodge No. 428 (Merchants Lodge), 1789. Liverpool Masonic Hall, Hope Street, Liverpool. Not listed.

List of Members & Minutes of the Lodge of Friendship, No.277, Oldham Masonic Hall, 1789-1900. Not listed.

Minutes from the Amicable Club, 1788-1803, Warrington Library, reference MS13.

Minutes from the Eagle & Child Club, 1781-1785, Warrington Library, reference MS14.

The Minute Books for the Mechanics Institute, 1838-1855, Warrington Library, reference MS235.

Minutes of the Lodge of Lights No.148, 1850-1900, Warrington Masonic Hall. Not listed.

Minutes of General Meetings of the Natural History Society, 1837-1853, Warrington Library, reference MS22.

Minutes of the Lodge of Harmony no. 220, 1822-1835, Garston Masonic Hall, Liverpool. Not listed.

Miscellaneous newspaper reports, Pennington, Leigh. Leigh Local Studies, WLCT. *Oddfellows Contribution Book, Loyal Orange Lodge no.143, 1835-42,* Warrington Library, reference MS280.

Reminiscences of an Unrecognized Lodge, namely Old Sincerity Lodge No. 486 by James Miller. Many thanks to the Rev. Neville Cryer who supplied the memoirs of James Miller. Not listed.

The Memoirs of Joseph Grime – a Rechabite from Platt Bridge, Wigan. Private Collection.

Various Collected Newspaper Reports of Provincial Grand Lodge Meetings, Warrington Masonic Hall, 1867 & 1869. Not listed.

Warrington Musical Society Documents: including the secretaries books, accounts, and list of members and subscribers 1833-1995, Warrington Library, reference MS2847.

Warrington School of Science Minute Book 1878-1884, Warrington Library, reference MS239.

Published Source Material

Anderson, James, *The Constitutions of The Free-Masons,* (London: Senex, 1723).

Anon., *Mysteries of the Independent Order of Foresters Unveiled, Or Trapped at the Alter of L.B.& C.,* (USA: Nabu Public Domain Reprints).

Bligh Bond, Frederick, *The Gate of Remembrance, The story of the psychological experiment which resulted in the discovery of the Edgar Chapel at Glastonbury,* (Kessinger Publishing Co., 1999).

Boswell, James, *Boswell's Life of Johnson,* (London: John Murray, 1847).

Cunningham, Peter, *Hand-Book of London, past and present,* (London: J. Murray, 1850).

Davies, J. A., (ed.), *The Letters of Goronwy Owen (1723-1769)*, (Cardiff: William Lewis Ltd, 1924).

Dickens, Charles, Jr., Dictionary Of London: An Unconventional Handbook, (London: Charles Dickens and Evans, 1879).

Duncan, Malcolm C., *Duncan's Masonic Ritual and Monitor*, (Forgotten Books, 2008).

Fenn, Thomas, The Prince of Wales's Lodge No. 259: list of members from the time of its constitution, (London: Jarrold & Sons Ltd., Revised ed. 1938).

Franklin, Benjamin, *The Autobiography of Benjamin Franklin*, (New York: Courier Dover Publications, 1996).

The Freemasons' Magazine: And Cabinet of Universal Literature For January 1796.

Gronow, Captain R.H., *Celebrities of London and Paris*, (London: Smith, Elder & Co., 1865).

Gronow, Captain R.H., *Reminiscences of Captain Gronow*, (London: Smith, Elder & Co., 1862).

Hamilton, C. W., *Degree Book – Order of Good Templars*, (The Right Worthy Grand Lodge of North America, 1858).

Hunt, Leigh, *The Town*, (Oxford: Oxford University Press, 1907).

Jupp, P., (ed.), *The Letter-Journal of George Canning, 1793-1795*, Royal Historical Society, Camden Fourth Series, Volume 41, (London, 1991).

Kipling, Rudyard, *Many Inventions*, (Kessinger Publishing Reprint, 2005).

Morgan, Owain, *Pabell Dofydd Eglurhad ar anianyddiaeth grefyddol yr hen dderwyddon Cymreig*, (Caerdydd: argraffwyd gan Daniel owen d'I ywmni, 1889).

Paine, Thomas, *Origin of Free Masonry*, in *The Works of Thomas Paine*, (New York: E. Haskell, 1854).

Stukeley, William, *Stonehenge a temple restor'd to the British Druids*, (W. Innys and R. Manby, 1740).

Viscount Leverhulme by his son, (London: Allen & Unwin Ltd., 1928).

Walesby, F.P., (ed.), *The Works of Samuel Johnson*, (Oxford: Talboys and Wheeler, 1825).

Walsh, Robert, (ed.), *Select Speeches of the Right Honourable George Canning with a Preliminary Biographical Sketch, and an Appendix of Extracts From His Writings and Speeches*, (Philadelphia: Crissy & Markley, 1850).

Warrington Trade Directories, 1792-1855, Warrington Library, reference S10121.

Warrington Examiner, 2 December 1916. Private collection. Not Listed.

Warrington Guardian, 22 September 1855. Private collection. Not Listed.

Wilde, Oscar, *The Complete Works*, (London: Magpie, 1993).

Yeats, W.B., 'The Secret Rose' in R.K.R. Thornton, (ed.), *Poetry of the 'Nineties*, (Middlesex: Penguin, 1970).

Secondary Works

Anon, *The Royal Antediluvian Order of Buffaloes Manual of Instruction*, (Leeds: Duffield Printers, 1983).

Anon, *Duke of Athol Lodge Bi-Centenary*, published by the Lodge, (1995).

Armstrong, J., *A History of Freemasonry in Cheshire*, (London: Kenning, 1901).

Armstrong, J., *History of the Lodge of Lights, no. 148*, (Warrington, 1898).

Arrowsmith, P., *Stockport - a History*, (Stockport MBC, 1997).

Baeza, Juan, *Restructuring the Medical Profession: The Intraprofessional Relations of GPs and Hospital Consultants*, (Maidenhead: Open University Press, 2005).

Bain, Ebenezer, *Merchant and Craft Guilds: A History of the Aberdeen Incorporated Trades*, (Aberdeen: Edmond, 1887).

Barrow, G., *Celtic Bards, Chief's and Kings*, (London: John Murray, 1928).

Barty-King, Hugh, *"Round Table" The Search for Fellowship 1927-1977*, (London: Heinemann, 1977).

Beesley, E.B., *The History of the Wigan Grand Lodge*, (Leeds: Manchester Association for Masonic Research, 1920).

Bennet, A., *A Glance at some old Warrington Societies*, (Warrington: Mackie & Co. Ltd, 1906).

Blocker, Jack S., Fahey, David M., and Tyrrell, Ian R., *Alcohol and Temperance in Modern History*, (ABC-CLIO Ltd., 2003).

Bullock, S.C., *Revolutionary Brotherhood*, (North Carolina: University of North Carolina Press, 1996).

Calvert, Albert F., 'Where Masons Used to Meet', in the *British Masonic Miscellany*, Compiled by George M. Martin, Vol. 20, (Dundee: David Winter and Son, 1936), pp. 95-98.

Carter, G.A., *Warrington Hundred*, (Warrington, 1947).

Crowe, A.M., *Warrington, Ancient and Modern*, (Warrington: Beamont Press, 1947).

Davie, Grace, *Religion in Britain Since 1945: Believing Without Belonging*, (Oxford: Wiley-Blackwell, 1994).

Evans, George Ewart, *Horse Power and Magic*, (London: Faber, 1979).

Evans, E. J., *The Forging of the Modern State: Early Industrial Britain 1783-1870*, (London: Longmans, 1992).

Faulks, Philippa and Cooper, Robert L.D., *The Masonic Magician; The Life and Death of Count Cagliostro and his Egyptian Rite*, (London: Watkins, 2008).

Fort Newton, Joseph, *The Builders*, (London: Unwin Brothers Limited, 1924).

Gee, B., *History of the Lodge of Friendship no.277*, (Oldham, 1989).

Gosden, P.H.J.H., *The Friendly Societies In England 1815-1875*, (Manchester: Manchester University Press, 1961).

Gould, R.F., *The History of Freemasonry, Vol. I-VI*, (London, 1884-7).

Greer, Mary K., *Women of the Golden Dawn; Rebels and Priestesses*, (Rochester, Vermont: Park Street Press, 1995).

Harland-Jacobs, Jessica, *Builders of Empire: Freemasonry and British Imperialism 1717-1927*, (North Carolina: North Carolina Press, 2007).

Harrison, David, *The Genesis of Freemasonry*, (Hersham: Lewis Masonic, 2009).

Harrison, David, *The Transformation of Freemasonry*, (Bury St. Edmunds: Arima Publishing, 2010).

Harrison, David, *The Liverpool Masonic Rebellion and the Wigan Grand Lodge*, (Bury St. Edmunds: Arima Publishing, 2012).

Harrison, David, *A Quick Guide to Freemasonry*, (Hersham: Lewis Masonic, 2013).

Harrison, David, *The York Grand Lodge*, (Bury St. Edmunds: Arima Publishing, 2014).

Hewitt, C.R., *Towards My Neighbour: The Social Influence of the Rotary Club Movement in Great Britain and Ireland*, (London: Longmans, 1950).

Hobsbawm, E. J., *Labouring Men*, (London: Weidenfeld and Nicolson, 1986).

Hyneman, Leon, *Freemasonry in England from 1567 to 1813*, (Montana: Kessinger Publishing, 2003).

Kelly, T., *A History of Adult Education in Great Britain*, (Liverpool: Liverpool University Press, 1970).

Kingsford, P.W., *Engineers, Inventors and Workers*, (London: Edward Arnold, 1973).

Klein, J. Herbert, *All About the Order of Elks*, (Los Angeles: International FA Publishing, 2011).

Longmate, N., *The Hungry Mills*, (London: Temple Smith, 1978).

Lovett, T., *Adult Education Community Development & The Working Class*, (Department of Adult Ed., University of Nottingham, 1982).

Mackey, Albert Gallatin, *A Lexicon of Freemasonry*, (London, 1869).

Mackey Albert Gallatin, and Haywood, H.L., *Encyclopedia of Freemasonry Part 1*, (Montana: Kessinger, 1946).

Macnab, John, History of The Merchants Lodge, No. 241, Liverpool, 1780-2004, Second Edition, (Liverpool, 2004).

Moran, Maureen, *Victorian Literature and Culture*, (New York: Continuum, 2006).

Nulty, G., *Guardian Country 1853-1978*, (Cheshire County Newspapers Ltd, 1978).

Oxford, A.W., *No. 4 an introduction to the History of the Royal Somerset House and Inverness Lodge*, (London: Bernard Quaritch Ltd., 1928).

Payne, M.W., *The Origin & Development of the Royal Antediluvian Order of Buffaloes*, (Leeds: John Blackburn Ltd., 1953).

Putnam, R.D., *Bowling Alone: The Collapse and Revival of American Community*, (New York: Simon & Schuster, 2000).

Putnam, R.D., *Democracies in Flux: The Evolution of Social Capital in Contemporary Society*, (New York: Oxford University Press 2002).

Rule, J., (ed.), *British Trade Unionism 1750 - 1850: The Formative Years*, (Longmans, 1988).

Saxelby, C. H., (ed.), *Bolton Survey (County History Reprints)*, (Bolton: SR Publishers, 1971).

Scholes, J. C., *History of Bolton*, (Bolton: The Daily Chronicle Office, 1892).

Solt-Denis, Victoria, *Discovering Friendly and Fraternal Societies: Their Badges and Regalia*, (Oxford: Shire Publications, 2008).

Stephens, W.B., *Adult Education And Society In An Industrial Town: Warrington 1800-1900*, (University of Exeter, 1980).

Surrey Dane, E., *Peter Stubs and the Lancashire Hand Tool Industry*, (John Sherratt and Son Ltd, 1973).

Tabbert, Mark A., *American Freemasons: Three Centuries of Building Communities*, (New York: New York University Press, 2005).

Tait, A., *History of the Oldham Lyceum 1839-1897*, (Oldham: H.C. Lee, 1897).

Thompson, E.P., *The Making of the English Working Class*, (Pelican, 1970).

Wood, Robert Leslie, *York Lodge No. 236, formerly The Union Lodge, the be-centennial history 1777-1977*, (York, 1977).

Woodford, A.F.A., Kenning's *Cyclopaedia of Freemasonry*, (London: Kenning, 1878).

Woods, Herbert, and Armstrong, James, *A Short Historical Note of Freemasonry in Warrington*, (Warrington, 1938).

Journals

Belton, John L., 'Masonic Membership Myths Debunked', in *Heredom*, Vol. 9, (Washington DC: Scottish Rite Research Society, 2001), pp. 9-32.

Belton, John L., 'Communication and Research versus Education' – the battle for a master mason's daily advance in Masonic knowledge', *AQC*, Vol. 118, (2006), pp. 210-218.

Burt, Roger, 'Industrial Relations In The British Non-Ferrous Mining Industry in the Nineteenth Century', in *Labour History Review*, Vol. 71, No. 1, (April 2006), pp. 57-79.

Durr, Andy, 'Chicken and Egg – the Emblem Book and Freemasonry: the Visual and Material Culture of Associated Life', in *AQC*, Vol. 118, (2006), pp. 20-36.

Fahey, David M., 'Why Some Black Lodges Prospered and Others Failed: The Good Templars and the True Reformers', in Matthew W. Hughey, (ed.), *Race and Ethnicity in Secret and Exclusive Social Orders: Blood and Shadow*, (London: Routledge, 2014), pp. 101-116.

Gould, R.F., 'English Freemasonry Before the Era of Grand Lodge', in *AQC*, Vol. 1, (1888), pp. 67-74.

Halstead, J., and Prescott, A., 'Breaking The Barriers: Masonry, Fraternity And Labour', *Labour History Review*, Vol. 71, No. 1, (April 2006), pp. 3-8.

Harrison, David, 'Freemasonry, Industry and Charity: The Local Community and the Working Man'. *The Journal of the Institute of Volunteering Research*, Volume 5, Number 1, (Winter 2002), pp. 33-45.

Harrison, David and Belton, John, 'Society in Flux' in *Researching British Freemasonry 1717-2017: The Journal for the Centre of Research into Freemasonry and Fraternalism*, Vol. 3, (Sheffield: University of Sheffield, 2010), pp. 71-99.

Jupp, P., (ed.), *The Letter-Journal of George Canning, 1793-1795*, Royal Historical Society, Camden Fourth Series, Volume 41, (London, 1991).

Klein, Lawrence, 'The Third Earl of Shaftesbury and the Progress of Politeness', *Eighteenth-Century Studies*, Vol. 18, No. 2, (Winter, 1984-1985), pp. 186-214.

Klein, Lawrence E., 'Liberty, Manners, and Politeness in Early Eighteenth-Century England', *The Historical Journal*, Vol. 32, No. 3, (September, 1989), pp. 583-605.

Mill, John S., 'The Corn Laws', in *The Westminster Review*, Vol. 3, (April 1825).

Money, John, 'The Masonic Moment; Or Ritual, Replica, and Credit: John Wilkes, the Macaroni Parson, and the Making of the Middle Class Mind', in *The Journal of British Studies*, Vol. 32, No. 4, (October, 1993), pp. 358-95.

Porter, George R., 'Free Trade', in *The Edinburgh Review*, Vol. 90, (July 1849).

Putnam, R.D., 'Bowling Alone: America's Declining Social Capital', in *Journal of Democracy*, Volume 6, Number 1, (Baltimore, Maryland, USA: Johns Hopkins University Press, January 1995).

Read, Will, 'The Spurious Lodge and Chapter at Barnsley', in *AQC*, Vol. 90, (1978), pp. 1-36.

Seemungal, L.A., 'The Rise of Additional Degrees' in *AQC*, Vol. 84, (1971), pp. 307-312.

Spurr, Michael J., 'The Liverpool Rebellion', in *AQC*, Vol. 85, (1972), pp. 29-60.

Starr, Martin P., 'Aleister Crowley: Freemason!', in *AQC*, Vol. 108, (1995), pp. 150-161.

Weinbren, Daniel, 'Mutual Aid and the Big Society', in *The Big Society Debate: A New Agenda for Social Policy?* (Cheltenham: Edward Elgar Publishing, 2012).

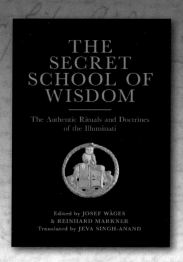